THE TOOLS OF OUR TRADE

The Heart of God's Way that Leads to Repentance

"The world doesn't fight fair. But we don't live or fight our battles that way—never have and never will. The tools of our trade aren't for marketing or manipulation, but they are for demolishing that entire massively corrupt culture. We use our powerful God-tools for smashing warped philosophies, tearing down barriers erected against the truth of God, fitting every loose thought and emotion and impulse into the structure of life shaped by Christ. Our tools are ready at hand for clearing the ground of every obstruction and building lives of obedience into maturity."

~2 Corinthians 10:3-4

Dedicated To:

Phil and Koral Chaney

Who took me on my first mission trip, and guided, developed, and nurtured my Love for missions, music and the tools in serving Jesus our Savior in truth through Authentic Worship, Lifestyle, and Love.

"A Legacy of Obedience, and to Press on."

TABLE OF CONTENTS

ACKNOWLEDGMENTS

First and foremost, I thank my Savior in Heaven. Only He made this book.

Thank you to my Mama and Daddy. Thank you for teaching me. Dad, I appreciate how I learned to have love for The Word and for ministry from you. Mom, thank you for giving me Romans 12:1-2 all those years ago, and for putting my first theology book in my hands.

To my brother, Nathan. I love you so much I can't stand it.

To my grandmothers, you inspire and love me too much! To my Grandma Nell who wrote me once a week while I was in Portland, I have kept every card. To my Grandmama Wiley, how many conversations have we had around your table with Your Bible and devotionals out in front of you? That's precious to me.

To my aunts who always listen and talk to me, and too have pointed me to Jesus, and to my uncles who are quiet but whom I watch, you have taught me so much about giving and loving.

To Koral Chaney, thank you for adopting me all those years ago to be your spiritual kid, and for pouring your life into me.

To my best friend and dearest sister in the Lord, Leslie. The late night phone calls, the never-ending conversations, and always being there for me. I love you and your family.

To Pastor Keith, and Beverly Evans at Greater Gresham in Oregon. Thank you for being my family in Oregon. My life is richer for knowing you.

To David and Barbara Prindle, more precious family in Portland, Oregon. I wouldn't have made it without you.

To Melanie and Joey Weaver, you've never stopped believing in me. I will always treasure our deep conversations and encouragement to write. Thank you for editing this book.

PROLOGUE

If there is one lesson God has taught me in life it is this: He holds my very life in His hands and sustains it every day with His breath. As God breathed life into Adam, He was showing us His personal involvement in our lives, in that He did not just speak us into being; He formed, He created, and then prepared us.   So it is with my life and with yours, too. He is the creator of life and the lover of life, and we are a reflection of His glory. [Colossians 1:15-20, John 1:1-18]

John tells us in his gospel that Jesus is the way, the truth, and the life, and that no man comes to the Father but through Him. Unfortunately, I failed to heed this truth for many years. However, this one thing I do know: even when I couldn't reach the Father, He has always been there holding my life in His hands, waiting for me to run to Him and find life. There have been many times in my short twenty-six years that haven't been so enjoyable and weren't seized as a gift. In fact, there have even been times I've wanted to end my life. I saw no purpose in it; I was a mistake, and everyone would be better off without me.

Thankfully, this wasn't how God saw things. I engaged in self-destructive behavior, but even in every rebellious act, God was there calling out to me. He held my life in His hands.

I grew slowly in my faith. In 2004, God gave me the gift of writing, from writing poetry, to songs, to letters, prayers, everything. Songwriting became a way to really build my relationship with Jesus. My songs tell my story and bare my heart. I began to read my Bible and put music to Psalms; I could relate to David's cries for help and understanding. Crying out is the beginning of revival. Writing became my outlet and a safe place.

In 2007, I moved to Charlotte with my family. I joined First Baptist Church Indian Trail, and God began to put me in specific places. It was there that I received strong teaching and guidance which pointed me in a much better and positive direction. I went on my first mission trip and loved it, and went on even more. I always had a particular interest in missions and had hoped that one day I would be able to do something like that. I joined the choir, I served in various ministries, where I met amazing spiritual giants of faith and locked in on watching them and their lives. I started to teach a Life Group; God opened many doors of opportunity. It wasn't long after that I developed a love for theology and studying my Bible and understanding who God really is. From theology stemmed a love for philosophy and then, a true love for the Word. Through my receiving His Word, God has set me free from so many bondages and addictions, thought patterns, and issues that hindered my Spiritual growth in Him.

The more I have surrendered and obeyed my Father in Heaven, the more He has trusted me with. I've noticed that when He reveals Himself to me, I can always go back to a hymn. The best theology can be found in the hymn book: "Great is Thy Faithfulness," "Trust and Obey," "I Surrender All," "How Great Thou Art," "Amazing Grace," "Blessed Assurance," "I Need Thee." It's not been an easy walk; the valleys have been low, the storms brutal and the lessons hard, but all along He has been there preserving my life, and the more I serve Him and grow in my relationship with Him, the better I see the path He is leading me down, and the calling He has on my life. I know He has anointed me with a special purpose.

On May 05, 2012, I surrendered to the call of ministry before the church. I wrote in my Bible, "Today, I commit myself to following His calling me into the ministry. Like Jonah, it is not too late to submit. My stubbornness is forgivable. Oh, depth of mercy, and grace from the Father; I trust Him and will not run anymore." However, God still had more to bring me through before He revealed His true calling for my life. All that year I searched and sought Him on the particular calling and work He had for me. God did a great work in my life that summer; I felt radically changed and redefined. In fact, I felt the Spirit's prompting to be baptized at our outdoor baptism. One year later, to the exact date almost, May 08, 2013, I realized God's calling of ministry on my life is to be a missionary, and He already had my first mission in place and ready for me to go; all I had to do was say "yes."

I can look back and see the hand of God and how He used certain people to prepare and train me to run with endurance. I was fortunate, blessed, and a better person to know Phil Chaney and to be under his leadership. Phil was a missionary; in fact, he called me his "little missionary." I learned so much about missions and loving others through him. I know God was preparing me by having me serve alongside him and watch his godly example, how he handled situations, and made decisions. The baton of this faith-race has been passed on, not just to me; it's been passed to you too. What will you do with it? I'm not where I need to be, but I know this much is true: I keep working toward that day when I will finally be everything Christ saved me for and wants me to be. Forgetting the past, and looking forward to what lies ahead. I strain to reach the end of the race and receive the prize for which God, through Christ, is calling us up to heaven. (Philippians 3:12-14)

INTRODUCTION

The sun shone through my window and woke me. My sinuses told
me that spring was in the air, and a great day in Portland to play
basketball—for two reasons. First, the sun was shining (which can be rare
in Portland), and second, it was actually warm enough to label the day
"Spring." When I was a kid, I had dreams of one day being a professional
basketball player. This sport was my passion; I loved the way they ball felt
in my hands, the way my heart would pound as I released the ball into the
air, waiting for it to go into the hoop. I will never forget the pep talk my
uncle gave me one evening. He sat me down and told me the skill and
passion I had for basketball would take me a long way if I only stuck with
it and did well in school. He promised me that he would be at every game
and would always cheer for me. He's an encourager, my uncle. His words
come back to me every time I pick up a basketball. I never made it to the
pros; I never played for Pat Summit at University of Tennessee. A dream
lost I suppose, but maybe not for the worse. I warmed up, and got to the
3-point line, bounced the ball a few times, stepped, planted my feet, eye
on the goal, exhaled, shot, followed through....*swish*. Repeat...bounce,

step, plant, goal, exhale, shoot, follow through...*miss*. Three hundred sixty times I did this. Then, God spoke to me. This is life. Sometimes we follow the exact formula and *swish*, but sometimes we miss, too. But we follow still, because it's the formula for how we live life well. Keeping my eyes on the goal (which is Christ), I step up to the line, plant my feet, breathe, shoot, follow through with the ball and either *miss* or *swish*. The team I surround myself with also makes a difference in my making the goal. If we are going to do well in life, we must have people on our team who will keep us moving toward the goal, and will do their best to ensure the ball goes in; people who will train alongside us and have their eyes on the same goal. People who will help keep our feet planted in the Word and in what is right and true. People who cheer us on and remind us to breathe.

The Bible teaches us that we are being trained in righteousness. No professional sports player is good just "because." There is a level of natural talent, yes, but most of them have a role model, a mentor who has held them accountable to maximize their potential. It's taken hours, months, and years of practice and training, of putting the body into submission. This is what we do spiritually, training our spirits into submission to God. We step up to the line of standard. We take the gifts

God has given us in our hands, and passionately and skillfully we shoot with everything we have in us for the goal God has set before us. (1 Corinthians 9:25, 1 Timothy 4:8 , Hebrews 12:11, 2 Timothy 3:16-17)

It's a small and simple thing, and it never occurred to me how important it is until I had to play without one: the net. It helps keep control of the ball, gripping it as the ball goes into the hoop. Oh yeah, and let's not forget to mention that satisfying "*swish*" sound! So it got me thinking, what is the net in my life? What controls me when I reach a goal, or even when I miss the goal? I love what my friend said: "we need to make sure we are letting God stay in control of our lives and let that 'swoosh' sound be our, 'Yes, and Amen, it's all because of Him.'" It's easy to start living without the net because it's so simple and small, like the still, quiet voice that gives us the cue that we made it....the strong right hand and the everlasting arms that keep us from slipping. It is the counsel He gives to keep us in the net, controlled, so we don't fly to the left or to the right, out of bounds. Is God controlling your life? If life feels like chaos at the moment and like you're flying all over the place, it's because you are and you need to get back in the net of the Holy Spirit's control. Or maybe you are meeting goals and still not feeling satisfied; you didn't hear the "*swish*." Get back in the net of knowing that it's only because of Jesus that you made the goal. He's the "Yes, and Amen."

While playing basketball when I was growing up, I was always positioned as a forward. I was out front, the first line of defense in keeping the opposing team from getting to the goal and scoring. I was tall, big boned, and strong, a good defense. Defense is what we use to keep Satan from adding people to his scoreboard. It is a gift God gave me to have an athletic build, but I had to learn to use certain parts of myself and train them in what they were supposed to do. We fit wherever God places us; sometimes we feel He crammed, pushed, and shoved us in, like square peg in a round hole.

In reference to the opening scripture of this book, there are two facets I want us to consider when we think of the word "trade." Consider what you do for a living, but look through the lens of God being a God who sends, and what you do really is missionary work. Yes, you on a mission for the sake of Jesus! Right where God has you. For some of us our "trade" and living is full-time ministry; we do it 24/7 and absolutely love it! We will come back to this toward the end, but for now, keep at the forefront of your mind the unique gifts, talents, and passions God has given to you, and how that may play into where He currently has you vocationally. As with any job or life situation really, we have tools we must learn to use. When it comes to spreading the Good News, we do not do it without first learning our game plan against the enemy and learning what our tools are. God has branded these tools in my life as I endeavored on my first missionary journey to the great city of Portland, Oregon. Where young people go to retire. Sadly I came out of retirement, but I will share some stories throughout the book. Portland is a very special city to me, and my time there was such a special experience; I hold it very closely to my heart. My love for the people in that land extends far and deep, and I am so thankful God sent me!

PART ONE:

I BOW LOW...

THE GIFT OF RIGHTEOUSNESS AND PEACE

CHAPTER ONE

Leave, Go, and Bless

"But you are the ones chosen by God, chosen for the high calling of priestly work, chosen to be a holy people, God's instruments to do his work and speak out for him, to tell others of the night-and-day difference he made for you—from nothing to something, from rejected to accepted."

1 Peter 2:9-10

We are a tool in the hand of God, chosen by His hand for the trade of speaking His truth. He decided before He laid the foundations of the world who we would be, what we would do, and how He would use us. This same God who saw us unformed, formed us in His love that we would be holy and without fault...imaged like Him; to be His, this is His will. It's hard for us to comprehend because we know who we are and who we've been.

God chose us to carry out His mission: to bring light to the World. When God shines His light on us, we find that it is a path leading to

Himself. We were not created to dwell in dark or live in doubt. When we

bury ourselves so deep to avoid hurts and sorrows, we wonder if God is

really enough? The shadow of doubt surrounds us; we have turned away

from the light. When we cast the shadow of doubt in our minds, we then

block the light of God's truth in our hearts. Jesus is the light of the world.

John 8:12 says, "Whoever FOLLOWS me will never walk in darkness."

While we may be weird and messed up in many ways, our focus can't

center on what we think, but instead what on what God is saying and

doing. He will allow us to experience trials so we can say for HIS glory

that He is faithful, and His promises are true. Feelings will always change,

but one truth is absolute, never changing, and that is our God. Here's

another truth: you are loved and chosen by the King! (Isaiah 43:4)

There is a verse in Matthew that says, "Many are called, but few

are chosen." Many hear the calling but few will respond in faithful

obedience to this calling. In the Greek, "calling" is defined as this: an

invitation to someone to accept responsibility for a particular task or a

new relationship. God calls/invites the believer to a relationship with Him

and to a particular role in His Kingdom. *Klesis* is the invitation itself, and

kletos describes a person who has already been called. We are called out by His commission to this spiritual warfare; we are chosen and fitted for it, and we must be faithful in it. When we respond to this calling, we are to live a life worthy of the calling. We are called and chosen to live a life of holiness. In the Old Testament, the Israelites had to sacrifice two lambs every day, it was public, bloody, smelly, and unpleasant in every physical way. It was not intended to please the participants, but to instill in the nation the horror of sin in the eyes of God and the absolute necessity of a substitutionary sacrifice.

In this choosing, we expect that He will have us do big things. There's a whole world out there! We experience excitement in the new and the adventure of following Jesus. Many will respond in resounding "YES!" to God; who would not want to see His wonders? With that choosing and calling, though, comes a life of being sanctified. Sanctification is a stripping away of the things in our life that don't please God. *"Purify yourselves, for tomorrow the Lord will do great wonders among you! Joshua told his people."* (Joshua 3:5). Repentance helps us live in that purifying. It is the blood of Jesus that makes us clean, His blood has covered our sin, and continues to.

In the Christian's life there is desecration or consecration, and we must constantly ask ourselves, which one am I giving myself to? I'm taken back to that old hymn:

Take my life, and let it be consecrated, Lord, to Thee.

Take my moments and my days; let them flow in ceaseless praise.

Take my hands, and let them move at the impulse of Thy love.

Take my feet, and let them be swift and beautiful for Thee.

When we are consecrated in the Lord, we are being sanctified, becoming more like Christ. God is calling us into His service; He is giving us glory and beauty. Desecration is the opposite. While we might be saved, we don't allow the Lord to live through us. We don't give ourselves fully to Him. It is the act of doing things that are not holy, and thus not living the life God desires us to have. Are you missing out on what He is doing? He is constantly working all around us. I pray for holy eyes that watch for Him with the expectation of witnessing the power of His hand at work. While we don't know fully today what He has in store for tomorrow, we wait obediently.

"A Godless city." That's how the city God was sending me to was being defined as in Christian terms. Would I leave my southern Bible Belt life to go and bless the people there? Why would He choose me for such a task?! What could this young southern belle do in a city where it is ranked Number Eleven among the most "post Christian" cities in America? As it is with all of America, we have turned away from God. However, God has and always will have a people! It's just up to those people to go and tell the world. God is the one who orders the steps of His children, not the world. We shouldn't get offended at the world; neither should we shout hate at the world. This has been the biggest lesson I've had to continuously learn. But I've had to learn it through the heart and eyes of Jesus, not the way the world presents "love" and "tolerance." The Bible has just the perfect story to show and prove, too. I have answered the call to be a missionary. Whether across the country, the world, wherever my feet go, the Spirit has led me through. I have found much guidance and teaching from the books and lives of Jonah and Nahum. I've been pondering and sifting through the jeweled truths over and over in my mind.

It is so amazing how God's message has never changed through the ages. The people and the problems we face have never changed through the ages either. The Bible is still as applicable today as it was 2,000+ years ago. There is nothing new under the sun; that's why, when you catch God's vision, and "above-the-sun" thinking, nothing is ever the same. Ninevah was founded by Nimrod, who we read about all the way back in Genesis 10:11. You'll remember Nimrod is the one who led the whole Tower of Babel building and rebellion against God. Ninevah is the capital of Assyria, and Assyria was the strongest of military leaders. No one dared fight them or try to destroy them. They saw themselves as invincible, and while they might have seemed unbreakable, they were a wicked city, and the stench of their sin was reeking to high heaven. While you may be wondering why God didn't just go ahead and destroy them in their wickedness and rebellion, this is where God is really revealing who He is. He loves all people, but not sin. God is a just God, his justice kept him from destroying them without first giving them the opportunity to repent and turn to Him. He already knew the outcome, but He was showing His grace and patience. So God sent His prophet Jonah on a mission to Ninevah with a message of judgement that if they did not repent and turn from the evil things they were doing, He would wipe them out. Yet, even God's chosen people mess up.

Jonah hated the Ninevites and wished God would go ahead and kill every last one of them; they deserved it! He ran the other direction. Even still, we see God in His character shine through. The whole theme of the Bible is redemption. In every story, you will encounter redemption, and will see that what Satan and man mean for bad, God turns it into something for His glory. GOD WILL BE GLORIFIED! In this we learn that we can never mess God up; we can never miss His will for our lives; no matter what mistakes and choices we make, He is in the business of redeeming. We may take detours, but if we wholeheartedly seek Him and answer Him when He calls, He will set us on the correct path.

On the boat in the last part of Chapter One, Jonah recognizes his sin, but also his other shipmates who were earlier praying to other gods recognized their own sin and the one true God Jonah worshiped, and as a result they were saved. It's never too late to submit; if He's calling and you have air in your lungs, answer.

After being thrown overboard, Jonah found he had his own repenting to do before the Lord. I love how it says in Chapter Two that Jonah, while inside the fish, cried out in prayer. Revival starts with you; it doesn't happen by going to church and expecting everyone else to change. I also love how Jonah saw that it was the Lord who threw him overboard; he didn't blame his friends. When Jonah finally made it to Ninevah on the "fish express," He preached God's judgement, and told them that if they did not repent and turn away from the godless things they were doing, God was going to destroy them. Deep in Jonah's heart though, he still wished God's wrath and judgement. However, something happened among the people; their eyes were opened, and dressing themselves in sackcloth they sat in ashes, beating their chest pleading for God to have mercy on them. None of us deserve God's forgiveness. It's amazing how Jonah knew who God was; he said, "I knew that you were compassionate and loving, gracious, slow to anger. I know how easily you would cancel your plans to destroy." How many times do we not do things because we know God and His character? "How dare God forgive that person," we say. Our focus must once more become God-centered and not self-centered. Jonah cried over his weed dying, but couldn't even muster up the tears to cry for the people who were about to be destroyed by God. When have we cried for the lost in our lives? We need to become sensitive to the spiritual needs of people and ask ourselves the very question God asked Jonah, "Is it right for you to be angry about this?" God ends the book of Jonah with these words: "Ninevah has more than 120,000 people living in spiritual darkness, not to mention all the animals. Shouldn't I feel sorry for such a great city?" I replaced "Ninevah" with Portland, the city God is sent me to.

CHAPTER TWO:

Humble Obedience

"If my people who are called by my name will humble themselves...and turn from their wicked ways..."

~2 Chronicles 7:14

For the majority of my life, I never knew what my purpose on Earth was. I didn't understand why God created me, and life was very confusing. I struggled through school with learning disabilities, didn't have friends, and I was a tomboy. I was always in trouble; most of that stemmed from my sense of independence and rebellion. I heard that verse in Jeremiah about God having a plan for me, and that He wanted to prosper me in good things. I remember moments and times of reaching out to God for help and having the desire to be better; my heart was longing, but my mind wasn't made up yet. I just didn't know how. Who was Jesus in me? Who was I in Him? How do I get these voices out of my head? For years I would stumble over these questions. In my first year of high school, my mom gave me this verse to memorize, since then I have claimed it as my life verse. Romans 12:1-2 says:

> "And so, dear brothers and sisters, I plead with you to give your bodies to God because of all he has done for you. Let them be a living and holy sacrifice—the kind he will find acceptable. This is truly the way to worship him. Don't copy the behavior and customs of this world, but let God transform you into a new person by changing the way you think. Then you will learn to know God's will for you, which is good and pleasing and perfect."

I would come to learn in studying these two verses tucked in Paul's letter to the Romans that this was Him in me, my spiritual worship, a verse that would lead to transformation, and a verse that was preparing me for the calling God was about to unleash on my life. I've always sensed God's hand of anointing on me, even in the days when I ran from Him, sowing wild oats and living however I wanted to.

This is one of the problems the children of Israel, God's chosen people had. They were going back and forth from believing that there was only one God to believing there were many gods. Though the God of Israel was with them and met with them, provided, directed, and loved

His children, they still rebelled. We can clearly see God among His people, pouring His love, protection, and blessing on them, yet, for some reason they would sacrifice to other gods, worship idols, and forget about the God who brought them out of bondage and slavery. Was their problem a faith problem? Or was it more of an obedience problem? It was both. It's not that they didn't believe in God, but that they didn't want to obey. If you were given the choice to live with one of the two people I'm about to describe who would you choose? The first is laid back, no standard, no boundaries, no expectations, and will let you live however you want. The second is strict, where there are standards to live by, and boundaries that are set, and you are expected to live in such a way that honors your family's name. This is what the nation of Israel, and even we today must answer. We are born with free will, and we can choose to serve gods and live "freely" with no rules or boundaries or, we can choose to serve the one true God, and live freely in who He is.

When we come to the end of Joshua, Israel has entered the Promised Land, conquering Jericho; they have fought many battles, witnessed the sun and moon stand still, and now Joshua is giving them their final orders before he dies. He knew the people of Israel and how they continuously kept worshiping idols:

14 "So fear the Lord and serve him wholeheartedly. Put away forever the idols your ancestors worshiped when they lived beyond the Euphrates River and in Egypt. Serve the Lord alone. 15 But if you refuse to serve the Lord, then choose today whom you will serve. But as for me and my family, we will serve the Lord." 16 The people replied, "We would never abandon the Lord and serve other gods. *17 For the Lord our God is the one who rescued us and our ancestors from slavery in the land of Egypt. He performed mighty miracles before our very eyes. As we traveled through the wilderness among our enemies, he preserved us. 18 It was the Lord who drove out the Amorites and the other nations living here in the land. So we, too, will serve the Lord, for he alone is our God." 19 Then Joshua warned the people, "You are not able to serve the Lord, for he is a holy and jealous God. He will not forgive your rebellion and your sins. 20 If you abandon the Lord and serve other gods, he will turn against you and destroy you, even though he has been so good to you." 21 But the people answered Joshua,*

"No, we will serve the Lord!" 22 "You are a witness to your own

decision," Joshua said. "You have chosen to serve the Lord." "Yes,"

they replied, "we are witnesses to what we have said."

23 "All right then," Joshua said, "destroy the idols among you, and

turn your hearts to the Lord, the God of Israel." 24 The people said

to Joshua, "We will serve the Lord our God. We will obey him

alone."

It's easy to slip into a quiet rebellion, going about life our own way. But

there comes a time when we must choose who and what controls our

minds and hearts. God or idols? Idol worship is easy; it's tangible! They

could see it, and it was surely easier to understand than this unseen God

who speaks from the sky. Seeing isn't always believing as the world

philosophies suggest. There are times when we have to believe in order

to see. Faith is the confidence that what we hope for will actually happen;

it gives us assurance about things we cannot see. And it is impossible to

please God without faith (Hebrews 11:1,6). It is our faith, though, that

wavers and causes us not to obey. And so all through the rest of the Old

Testament, idolatry continued across generations. The people did what

was right in their own eyes. Today, we do have a King, and His name is

Jesus. Faith willingly obeys, because it is a faith that has seen and heard. God did not speak for 400 years between the book of Malachi and Matthew! 400 years! Why?! I think because of idolatry. There comes a point where God will leave us in our sin because we have free will (Romans 1:28-32), and we have made our choice. How hopeless that must be. Can you imagine? How many generations passed not ever hearing from God?

We come to this generation now. God's will isn't so difficult to follow or be in, not nearly as difficult as we think or make it out to be. All this frantic searching leaves us in a mess and with no peace; this in itself isn't God's will. Our problem is that we do not absolutely surrender our lives. Only when we stop seeking after ourselves and seek Him will we cease to live in discontent and worry. There can only be one will between God and ourselves Paul says so in 1 Corinthians 3. So the real question becomes, "Who is my master?" In this aspect our ways, actions, and choices are determined, and that is what we are asking when we pray for His will to be done; we are praying for His specific plan and purpose in the things we do. We want to know the will of God, but often don't take the time to know the One who is the "will giver." We tend to seek more after the "will" than we do the Father. It is the Father who leads to the will, because His heart is where it's found. Oh that we would be like David and be men and women after God's own heart. We truly discover and experience God when we get desperate for Him. It's a commonality found all throughout the Bible; in every great story told is a man who is desperate before God.

Desperation is a humble place. It is a result of the Refiner's fire, where these earthen vessels are tried and tested. It's one of the tools God uses to get us into His will. We wave the white flag of surrender, and desperately we cry out to God and know that if He doesn't show up, we're not going to make it. We ask, "God, what are we going to do?!" Because we don't know the answers anymore; we don't have anyone else to call on, and we have no more words we can say. Then God, in His rich love and compassion, does something miraculous.

It had long been foretold that a shoot from David's tree would come as the King forever. In the deafening, long, and painful silence of 400 years, God broke through and introduced His son, Jesus, as a baby's cry. There He was, tangible, visible, just what the world had been holding its breath for. How uncomfortable is that?! Expecting royalty to come in and save the day, and he turns out to be helpless baby born to a teenager. That wasn't the plan everyone was looking for. But He came as Emmanuel and the Prince of Peace so that we may be the receiver of His righteousness. In great humbleness, He became human so that I in my humanness might become like Him. Paul says in 1 Corinthians 5:21: "For He made Him who knew no sin to be sin for us, that we might become the righteousness of God in Him." I have learned that selfless giving is the way into a person's heart. Jesus knew this too. It is the act of humbly submitting ourselves to another in love. In a world that is selfish, selfless giving is shocking and radical. Sometimes selfishness can even be disguised. Things we as Christians would never label as being selfish suddenly take us away from opportunities to give to another.

Such a thing happened to me in Portland. Sometimes I forget that it's okay to have a life outside of the walls of church and "churchy" things. I drove to Starbucks where the Lord gave me two opportunities (just as I had asked Him earlier that day), to minister to people. Ministry happens outside of the walls of the church building too. The guy behind the counter was new to the area, so I invited him to the church where I was interning. I placed my order, and he was so helpful and patient with me as I scrambled to figure out what I wanted. The lady behind me ordered

her drink as I stood there waiting for my drink to be made. The Spirit then

moved me to pay for her drink, and she was grateful and shocked. I mean

let's get real here, it's rare that a complete stranger wants to pay for your

order. In talking to her and learning her story, I came to find out that her

birthday was the next day. In that moment, though I wasn't able to share

the gospel, I know I planted a seed that God will bless and begin to

cultivate.

Jesus did the same thing. But He did more than just buy us a cup

of coffee. He humbled Himself, carried the cross and died upon it. On it,

the sin of the world was placed on Him, and once and for all He died for

every sin that would ever be committed. He gave His life. On top of it all,

He was innocent. Jesus had done no wrong; He had never committed a

sin. That's as selfless as you can get! The decision to follow and accept

Jesus is selfless as well, because a life of following Him bids us to come

and die to ourselves, take up our own cross, and follow in His footsteps. It

means we are to become servants to those who surround us. It means

doing the things that not most everyone wants to do. Jesus washed the

feet of His disciples; He hung out with the sinners and avoided the religious folks. Isn't that interesting? When we read the Bible, most of where Jesus was found is not in the temple, but in His community meeting people where they were. That is not to say Jesus neglected His Father's house, but He reached out to those who needed Him the most. I think that's where I find myself often: caught up in religion....wanting to hang out at church more than I want to hang out with the people who need to see and experience the light of who Jesus is in me, those who need to experience His love, His peace, His contentment, His hope, His joy....This is what I mean by being selfish and not even knowing it. It is when we stay in our comfort zone, within the walls of the church with people just like us, and never reach out to the outside world where Jesus has sent us that we fail to deliver His message. And it's not only the message of the Gospel, but the message of who He is; it is what lives in us.

I pray to become more aware of the things God is putting before me, that I would seize the opportunities I ask Him for in the first place! That I would quit getting caught up in religion and doing what I think is right, and instead do what the Father tells me is right and be where I need to be. I believe this is what it means in my life-verse when it says to offer yourselves as a living sacrifice. It's doing the things that wouldn't be our first choice and humbly laying our lives down, pouring ourselves out before Him and before the people He loves and has called according to His purposes. This is the path to righteousness. There is no other way or path I would rather walk in, and there is no other way God leads His children than in paths of righteousness for HIS name's sake.

In the Greek, the definition of righteousness is "the character of being right or just." It is unattainable by obedience to any law or by any merit of man's own or any other condition than that of faith in Christ. We can never be what God requires us to be; only by His son Jesus and by receiving Him through faith are we able to walk in the ways of the Lord. We can't be obedient without righteousness. In that moment of the mind and the spirit accepting Jesus as our Lord through faith, we immediately identify with Him in humility and become conformed to His will.

When it comes to the fight against the world attempts to make us fit in and the fight against Satan for our souls and others around us, we put on The Breastplate of Righteousness; we're covered by the blood, and our hearts belong to Jesus. Satan might come in and gain a foothold, but it won't be for long if Jesus has residence there. This is a matter of living in the flesh versus living in the Spirit. The Christian life is not centered on spiritual warfare, but on the joyful life of obedience in the Spirit; this is a life centered on Christ and on the finished work of the cross. The cross demands a new lifestyle. The Spirit who wrote the Word is the influence. What steps we take will be influenced by the Word through the Holy Spirit.

The armor we have on protects us. It doesn't make us invisible to war and attack though; it isn't a bubble, so it doesn't mean that you put it on and then Satan leaves you alone. We are going to get the wind knocked out of us because we belong to Jesus. The cross has become glamorous; I think the armor has been made to look glamorous too. It isn't gold-plated and ready for a show. The cross and the armor are tools, covered in blood, sweat, flesh, and vomit, because it has been in war. I believe we must begin to ask ourselves ever so often, "What does my Armor look like today?" **Our armor will always match the cross we look to. Either the old rugged cross Jesus died upon, or a gold-plated idol.**

He's shifting my heart from expecting to enter the Promised Land to only getting to see it from a distance. God lets someone else experience it. This can seem unfair to our flesh, because we think, *God, didn't we sacrifice, didn't we invest, didn't we risk and sell it all? Didn't we hang out and lead these rebellious people through this desert? Didn't we pray faithfully? Isn't it our heart that is burdened and ready to receive? Where is the reward?!* Here's a lesson of truth: God always has a deeper reason and a direction He is trying to take us. In my frustration over being the "sower" and not necessarily the "reaper of the harvest," I wonder if I'm elevating Portland above God....am I worshiping what I'm praying for? I think that's easy to do. We can get so attached to a situation or burden that it takes our heart's throne. How do we make these requests and burdens bow to God? Isn't He the one that owns it all? He can do whatever He wants; we just have to let Him. We all hope to leave a legacy when we die. What will we be remembered for? Whose lives did our lives connect with and impact? Did we really even make a difference at all? I knew a man who did just that; he left a legacy of obedience, fulfilling the call and mission God had given him. Through his obedience, God used his life greatly to impact thousands of people. A legacy of obedience begins with a trust that believes our faith will lead us through this life to Heaven with an overwhelming joy that cannot be explained even unto death. It is a supernatural love given by the Holy

Spirit within us that compels us to walk worthy in the Father's way.

CHAPTER THREE:

When I Mention His Name

"If my people who are called by my name will humble themselves and pray and seek my face and turn from their wicked ways, I will hear from Heaven and will forgive their sins and heal their land."

~2 Chronicles 7:14

I don't know if you've noticed, but our land is in need of peace. We are threatened by ISIS, riots in our street, terrorism, corrupt government; the list could go on and on. It's hard to know what to pray for. Is peace even attainable at this point in our world? This is the wrong question to be asking. God's peace is different than what we would define as peace. When we pray for God's peace, we ask Him to step into our chaos and give it order, to make our relationships with people harmonious, that we would be content, to give us rest, to bring quiet. We desire a place where there is justice, grace, and no sadness.

This is the peace through salvation; this is what we are given to spread to the world around us and to the ends of the earth. This peace is the peace that snatched us from death to life; it's peace in a place where Satan once claimed dominion but now belongs to the sons and daughters of God. We are sent out in the world to spread peace. The prophet Isaiah proclaimed, "How beautiful are the feet of those that bring Good News." It all points to Salvation. God's justice in the world is when righteousness and peace kiss, when right living kisses redemption. Psalm 85 is a beautiful picture of this:

> "Will you prolong your wrath to distant generations? I listen carefully to what God the Lord is saying, for He speaks peace to His people, His faithful ones. But let them not return to their foolish ways. Surely His Salvation is near to those who honor Him; our Land will be filled with His glory. Righteousness and peace have kissed! It goes as a herald before Him..." (vs. 5, 8-10, 13)

Israel had prayed for God's peace in and out of exile. We pray for peace to come throughout the world with the message He has given us to share. We pray for the bond of peace in our churches, both locally and globally. (Ephesians 4) The Good News of Jesus is the balm that brings healing. If you read Isaiah 59, it doesn't read too differently from today's newspapers concerning our nation and even our churches! We are calling out for God to save us, and when He doesn't, we doubt His existence. Israel was in the same boat. God didn't reach down because the hearts of a generation and people remained unrepentant. If we want to bring the culture we are trying to reach to repentance, then we must first repent. We must repent of our own personal sin, for sin of the church, for not standing in the truth and in the authority of Heaven. We must repent for the sin of our country, for not standing on the rights God gave us in freedom and liberty, and justice that reflected Himself. Are we a broken people? Do we intervene in prayer for the lost? Do our hearts hurt to hear statistics that tell of a lost generation, of a culture that celebrates everything that is so wicked in the sight of God, and even takes pride in it? They are not looking to the God of justice but have made in their own eyes a god of tolerance and exceptions. When Isaiah repented of the nation's sin, God responds with redemption. In this prophets book,

*"The Lord looked and was displeased to find there was no justice. He was amazed to see that **no one intervened** to help the oppressed. So he himself stepped in to save them with his strong*

arm, and his justice sustained him. He put on righteousness as his body armor and placed the helmet of salvation on his head. He clothed himself with a robe of vengeance and wrapped himself in a cloak of divine passion." (Isaiah 59: 15-17)

Simply the mention of His name calls Him to intervene. Salvation is wrapped in mentioning His name. The original Hebrew word is *zakar*; it means to remember, think of, or mention. It also indicates that a response to a need or situation will occur, implying a relationship or a renewal of an old relationship. It implores us to remember our salvation, to remember the one who rose; the source and supplier, not implying in a way that we forgot or don't know, but that we should keep in mind who God really is.

Who will intervene in prayer? Who will mention His name? Our prayers cause us to gaze upon the Creator. When we pray humbly and obediently, our hearts align with His, and our lips are praying what His heart is praying. We experience His presence, and He refreshes our weary souls entering into His rest that is salvation.

It wasn't very long that I had been at my job in Portland that I was promoted to being an Opening Supervisor. That would mean I would have to be at work really, really early, and my job would include standing at the industrial sink for a really, really long time washing dishes, machine parts, and containers. During this time, I would be at the shop alone until my boss or crew would come in, and I found myself using the time to pray. It was quiet, and God just started speaking to me as I did my duties. It wasn't anything I initiated; it just became a place where God began to meet me. I have realized what a sacred thing that was and how cool it was that Jesus would come and meet me at a sink at work. For so long I used to think that when I met with God I needed to be in this corner, or some little space the Bible calls a prayer closet, with lots of crosses around me, and spiritual sayings, and Jesus things, and that I would have this great feeling fall over me and "feely" stuff like that, and that I would have to pray for a certain amount of time. My, have I been wrong. Jesus has met me at an industrial sink...just me and Him. I caught myself smiling and laughing randomly as He whispered sweet things over me, bringing memories and people to mind who were back home that I missed so badly. As I stood over the sink washing, elbow deep in JOY dish soap, I asked Jesus to wash me too, to clean the dirty things out of life and to restore joy to those areas. One of my other jobs included **making hot** fudge. If made correctly, it doesn't spoil before it should, and everything about it is perfect; it tastes good, and it's smooth. Getting it this way takes work, though. It's not as simple as simply opening a can. We stir, fold, and patiently work it until it eventually comes together and becomes the finished product that is ready to serve. This reminded me of how God has us in a mixing bowl. Patiently He stirs us, adding the correct ingredients to our lives, making us the perfected product He wants in the end for the purpose of serving other people. Many times we get aggravated with ourselves, and if you are like me you keep asking yourself, "Why can't I ever be good enough?" "What more do I need to do?" There are times where all we can do is just stay in the mixing bowl, letting God stir our hearts. He is the one who makes us all He wants us to be. The easiest way to get distracted from the mission of God is to determine our own mission and invest in it. It's like we jump out of the mixing bowl and give up on God. We conclude that He screwed up and now we have to fix it all. He's still adding ingredients to do His mission. The full life, the one spilling joy and peace, happens only as I come to trust the caress of the Lover; the Lover who never burdens His children with shame and guilt, but keeps firmly stroking their fears with gentle grace. He teaches, crafts, and molds in the most unique ways.

How is it that sacred ground can be the very places in our lives where we kind of dread standing? Washing dishes isn't so fun most of the time; how many times have I fought my parents on that?! I can't even get them done at my own house!! Making hot fudge wasn't fun either. Isn't it interesting how God takes places that are hard in our lives and makes them a place of worship? A place of sacrifice. An altar. Sacred Ground. Unlikely places. Where is the holy ground? How do we make everything in our lives bow and serve our God? Our workplaces can be a place of worship. We can either worship our job, or make it worship God. How do we make it worship God? He can meet you where you are. That's been really powerful for me. If our hearts are after Him, He will speak.

The story of Jehoshaphat has been a meaningful message in my life over the past several years, especially in the context of worshiping in the face of adversity. When the armies of the Moabites and Ammonites declared war against King Jehoshaphat and his people, right then Jehoshaphat prayed standing "before the people of Judah and Jerusalem at the temple of the Lord"(v.5). He prayed, "Whenever we are faced with any calamity such as war, disease, or famine, we can come to stand in your presence before this temple where your name is honored. We can cry out to you to save us, and you will hear us and rescue us."(v.9) What we tend to do with God is ask him to take care of something but not want to do anything ourselves. We just want to sit on the bench and watch. It's still your problem; God will work through us when we praise him, and when we allow him to use us. The Spirit of The Lord came upon the men and answered Jehoshaphat's prayer saying: "Do not be afraid! Don't be discouraged by this mighty army, for the battle is not yours, but God's. Tomorrow march out against them….but you will not need to even fight. Take your positions; then stand still and watch the Lords victory. He is with you."(v.15-18) "Early the next morning the army of Judah marched out toward the battlefield, with king appointed singers walking ahead, singing to the Lord praising him for his holy splendor. The hymn they sang, 'Give thanks to the Lord, for His faithful love endures forever.' At that moment when they began to sing and praise, the Lord caused the armies of Ammon, Moab, and Mount Seir to fight and kill among themselves. Not a single one of the enemy had survived."(v.20-24).

Something to notice about worship outlined in this passage is that worship begins when the Spirit of the Lord falls upon us. He is the initiator of worship. Just because your mouth moves and sings a few verses doesn't always mean you encounter God face to face. Worship isn't anything we create or force, not if it's authentic. It might be an acceptable worship style, but authentic worship occurs when our lives depend on it like the very air we breathe.

Worship is about being present, about showing up to the places where we may find Him, just like my standing at the industrial sink washing dishes. Where He is present, we must be present too. Where is He working? Where is His hand moving? It's about getting in on what God is doing; we're on the edge of our seats watching and waiting.

We notice worship is a position. It is becoming aware of ourselves before an Almighty God; it's knowing that He is to be honored. We humbly bow before Him and declare that God alone is the head of the soldiers. Our position is to be still at times; other times it's to march.

When we believe God in our circumstances, a joyful noise leaves our lips to His ear and heart. The Hebrew word used for praise is *halal;* it is a verb that means "speaking excellence of something or someone," whether to a false god, or the one true God. What is more excellent in our life; what do we speak of more? What comes out of our mouth is where our belief lies. The people of Judah and Jerusalem sang, "Give thanks to the Lord, his faithful love endures forever!"

Worship confuses the enemy. If you know your enemy, Satan, the reason He started his whole rebellion against God was because nobody was worshiping him. He wanted to be the highest in Heaven. He wanted himself exalted. He wanted the throne. When we stop giving Satan praise, and only praise God, Satan doesn't want much to do with that; he'll go find the next person who will give him the time of day.

So what are your gifts? Who are you in this story? Do you have strong leadership skills? Do you love singing? Are you an encourager who keeps those around you marching forward? Do you have a gift of being a prayer warrior? The most important thing is to remember to give God the glory, and not ourselves, or Satan in the use of our gifts.

CHAPTER FOUR

Repentance

"Jesus said, 'I have come to call sinners to turn from their sins, not to spend my time with those who think they are already good enough.'"

~Luke 5:32

We are born with "self" on the throne of our hearts. This is the decision maker of who we are. Martin Luther said, "I more fear what is within me than what comes without." We can believe in God, but if asked if we are innocent or guilty we would have to answer "guilty." Romans 3:23 states that, "All have sinned, and fall short of God." Since the fall of man, sin entered our blood, and the result has been a nature that thinks impure thoughts, and envies, fights and bickers with others. This is what our flesh produces. John Murray is quoted as saying, "Sin does live in me, but I don't have to live in sin." To the believer, we live in Christ Jesus, who is our Lord and our Savior. Jesus is the Word, as John 1 teaches, so we are also living in the Word of God. In it He tells us how not to sin so much. It is said often in scripture that what comes out of the heart is indicative of the person. Scripture also encourages us to hide His Word in our hearts that we might not sin against God. The more we are in His Word and applying it, the more we are changed moment by moment. This is living a life yielded to Christ, and as a result of the Holy Spirit controlling our life, we produce love, joy, peace, patience, kindness, and faithfulness. We aren't always feeling this. Vines Dictionary defines repentance as this: "The action or condition of change, especially of behavior and opinions. Changing from sinful state to a righteous standard. Change of perspective that results in changed actions."

It is important that we know we cannot go back to our old self; that person died. We are now a new creation. We will keep messing up and falling back into old habits, but they are habits only Jesus can break. This can take time. There will be times when we aren't feeling so Spirit-filled, but be assured that He has not left us; we've just taken over again with self. This is a constant battle. Sin led us back, but Jesus is stronger, and He loves us too much to leave us there; He comes after us! In doing so we humble ourselves before Him, taking ourselves off the throne, and enthroning Him once more. Fellowship is restored when we repent.

Through repentance we obtain forgiveness and release from sin. This makes repentance a gift. We cannot repent on our own terms; God convicts and brings the opportunity just as He does in our salvation. In the same way, He is patient. We may reject His calling us to Himself; He gives us lots of chances. Until there is repentance, we are on unstable ground because our knowledge of the truth has shifted; sin causes us to be in opposition of the truth. Sin is not truth. Every time we repent and turn our backs on Satan, we are laying a foundation and building a life that reflects Jesus. When we give our lives to Jesus and believe in Him as Savior, we realize the sin in our lives and our need for Him. Jesus cleaned us up and gave us clean clothes; clothes that fit us, and He continues to change us "from glory to glory," as Paul says.

I love the story told in Zechariah 3:

Then the angel showed me Jeshua the high priest standing before the angel of the Lord. The Accuser, Satan, was there at the angel's right hand, making accusations against Jeshua. **2** *And the Lord said to Satan, "I, the Lord, reject your accusations, Satan. Yes, the Lord, who has chosen Jerusalem, rebukes you. This man is like a burning stick that has been snatched from the fire."*

3 Jeshua's clothing was filthy as he stood there before the angel.4 So the angel said to the others standing there, "Take off his filthy clothes." And turning to Jeshua he said, "See, I have taken away your sins, and now I am giving you these fine new clothes."

5 Then I said, "They should also place a clean turban on his head." So they put a clean priestly turban on his head and dressed him in new clothes while the angel of the Lord stood by.

6 Then the angel of the Lord spoke very solemnly to Jeshua and said, 7"This is what the Lord of Heaven's Armies says: If you follow my ways and carefully serve me, then you will be given authority over my Temple and its courtyards. I will let you walk among these others standing here.

I love the picture that is being painted. A brand new outfit makes you feel brand new doesn't it? We're the King's kids now; we must dress the part in the new, clean clothes the King has given us right in front of Satan. Satan does not give us anything new; he drags us through the mud and eventually throws us in our grave. More importantly, people will recognize we have authority by what we have on. It's how we recognize who people are and what they do. We recognize a policeman by the uniform he has on and the tools he carries.

I'll never forget the first time I went to Portland; I desperately needed a new pair of tennis shoes. I'd been praying for a new pair-- specifically NIKES, because every athlete's choice is NIKE. Of course, any pair of tennis shoes would have made me grateful and happy. A lady in the church I was serving at took me to a NIKE outlet and bought me a new pair, and I loved them! I prayed over my new pair of tennis shoes and committed them to the Lord to do His work. Every new morning, I woke up thankful for new mornings, NIKES, and feet that move to bring Good News!

PART TWO:

I LIVE ABOVE THE SUN

THE GIFT OF SALVATION AND FAITH

CHAPTER FIVE

Evangelical Wisdom

"Since you have been raised to new life with Christ, set your sights on the realities of heaven, where Christ sits in the place of honor at God's right hand. 2Think about the things of heaven, not the things of earth. 3For you died to this life, and your real life is hidden with Christ in God. 4And when Christ, who is your life, is revealed to the whole world, you will share in all his glory."

~Colossians 3:1-4

In my observation of the church and how missions is handled, I've noticed that we get in the way a lot, and I say "we" because I'm more in the way than a herd of cows in the highway. *Mooooove.* Freely speaking the convictions of my heart, I fear for this generation and how "mission" seems to have become a buzz-word. I do not speak from a critical or judgmental attitude; I speak from observations made. I worry when I see pictures from the missional organizations that I follow being presented as more of an "outing" than an "outreach." My fear is that missions are becoming trendy, making Jesus and the cross trendy, a new hashtag. I'm not labeling this "bad" or "sin"; I'm labeling it as a red flag that goes up in my heart. Because all trends eventually come to an end, and people don't need a new trend or a new thing to hashtag. What people need is the Ancient of Days, the one who has been "trending" before time. Is missions our new entertainment? A trend, hashtag, or entertainment will not keep you alive on the mission field.

Knowing Jesus is forever. We live in a culture that is dying to live, a generation that shouts "YOLO" (you only live once) whose mindset is living life something fierce, chasing the American dream, experimenting, pushing limits, all in the name of living the one life they hold in utmost regard to all others. There is a war of pride that covers like a cloud, causing spiritual darkness in our cities and across the globe. It is a result of generations not seeking to obey God, but remaining in a rebellious state against all authority. The church has been given the mission to meet our culture and generation and to take back what is God's. We are in a battle for every soul purchased by the blood of Jesus...it's the world!

I found Jesus in the book of Ecclesiastes; I will never forget what a season of life change that was. Is there meaning to life? Yes! But you have to look in the right place, or more so, the right person. In this life it's not about what you know, but who you know. Our Creator, God, made us with eternity set in our hearts. It's that feeling "YOLO" stems from, that something needs to be fulfilled, that constant nagging feeling of wanting something more. We dream and dare to live fully and do big things. But what if we are already living the dream and living fully? What are we missing that is right in front of us? How do we live like we are dying? It's not found by taking huge trips across the globe or jumping off a cliff, or swimming with sea turtles, or anything else that might be on the "bucket list." It's found in our average day-to-day life. How is God revealing Himself to you? How does He want you to embrace Him? We go through life mumbling, "if only!" But what do you have now? Thankfulness is the royal road to draw near to Him. A thankful heart has plenty of room for Jesus. When we thank Him, we affirm that He is God, the provider from whom all blessings flow. When we thank Him for the hard stuff, we trust His sovereignty. My spiritual mother taught me this too. "Every trial and tribulation is adding adornment for the wedding dress I marry Jesus in." Why would I not thank Him for the beauty he makes out of ashes? He is preparing us for Himself. *"To all who mourn in Israel, he will give a crown of beauty for ashes, a joyous blessing instead of mourning, festive praise instead of despair. In their righteousness, they will be like great oaks that the Lord has planted for his own glory."* -Isaiah 61:3

I was at a leadership conference sponsored by Lifeway. Toward the end of the session, we did an exercise where we went outside and sought out an object that we felt best described our life in Christ at that moment. We had about fifteen minutes to complete the task. Prayerfully, I walked around reflecting and allowing the Lord to show me myself and what item best suited me. I came across a lid; am I screwed up? Of course, but that wasn't it. On I walked. A leaf? A blade of grass? Firewood...I stood for a moment, and stared at it, it felt right. But on I walked, to think about it and to see if anything else might be better. No, that was it, a piece of firewood. I picked it up...yeah...I'm a piece of firewood. In I walked; I think I had the largest item. God showed me many things in this piece of firewood. He is still carving me out to be something valuable and beautiful. At times, I'm thrown in the fire, and need to catch onto the fire of the Holy Spirit. I am burned down to ash. My friend reminded me that it too is beauty; He gives beauty for ashes. I was also amazed to learn on my cross country trip that forest fires can be beneficial. They burn away the old and fertilize the ground for new growth. We approach seasons of newness and growth. Fires of life produce growth and fertilize the ground

for new things.

Our eyes must be shifted from self to God. And just like the

middle of a doughnut, He must become the center of our being. It is

through Him that life becomes more than aging or trying to get the most

out of life because "this is it." He is the hope of Heaven that causes us to

sing, "Whatever my lot, He's taught me to say, It is well with my soul."

Ecclesiastes is Solomon's repentance of the "YOLO" life.

Remember, Solomon was the one who, back in the book of 2 Samuel

when God said to him, "Ask of me anything and I'll give it to you," asked

for wisdom, and because of his request God granted it to him, but He also

gave him great riches. Solomon had it all: endless partying, women, and

rock concerts. Solomon's main message is that everything you can think

to do under the sun is absolutely meaningless if it cannot be done to the

glory of God. Only when we live life God's way and for "that day" will this

life have meaning. Live for Heaven, above the sun.

Evangelism is preaching salvation; it is the Greek word *soterion.* It

means telling of the future deliverance of believers at the presence, arrival, and official visit (*parousia*) of Jesus Christ which is the object of confident hope and assurance of deliverance in the outpouring of God's wrath at the end of this age. Our purpose in evangelism points to the "day of the Lord." And when we face Satan in warfare we know that we know, we are saved and have this confident hope that Jesus is our deliverer both in this day and on that day. (1 Cor. 1:8, 1 Thess. 5:2, 2 Thess. 2:2, 2 Peter 3:10, Rev. 20:7-15)

Today, it is not uncommon to see young people wear colored bracelets and wristbands, and some have a word or words written on them. If you grew up in the 90's, then you remember well the WWJD bracelet, am I right?! It is worn to promote or remind you, or to give you something to make conversation about. I had a conversation with a young man at the Starbucks I frequented in Portland. I saw him across the room; he was wearing a black bracelet with large white font that read "BELIEVE." Thinking he may be another fellow believer in Christ and maybe a potential friend, I left my seat and made my way to him. I started the conversation by telling him, "I like your bracelet." He invited me to sit down, and we discussed what the meaning of his bracelet was to him. He told me a friend of his gave it to him because he has strong beliefs and convictions. I asked him what they were. His beliefs consisted

of different pieces of religions put together, creating what he liked and

accepted. He didn't believe in Hell, but instead believed that Earth was

hell. He put humans on the same supreme level with Jesus Christ. He

didn't believe a good God would send people to Hell. Oh yes, my friend

had beliefs, but they weren't eternal and had no object. We can be

hopeful and we can have beliefs, but can still be missing something and

someone. There must be an object, a living object, that we tie our belief

and hope in and to. Only Jesus. He is the one who is Hope. He is the one

we believe.

Do you know where your treasure is? If Heaven is our aim first,

then earth becomes a gift, but if earth is all we aim for, we become its

slave. From a missional standpoint, God's kingdom should be every

believer's aim, what we devote our lives to. There is an order to building

the kingdom. It begins with letting the words of Jesus through His Word,

the Bible, have a forever home in our hearts so that we may become

wise, using His words to disciple and build up others (Colossians 3:16).

Take inventory of who you surround yourself with, because it's who you

become like. Everyone should be discipling another. I have these mentors in my life. They are the people who will hold you accountable to the standard of Jesus Christ. I love all who God has given me and allowed to pour into my life. They are relationships that compel, encourage, and strengthen me because we are better together.

This can lead to some pretty uncomfortable seasons in life. But living to the standard of Jesus and to His mission of bringing Good News to the ends of the Earth was never promised to be comfortable. The ends of the Earth can be pretty dark, and you may be the only little light that shines. We must shine gracefully even in uncomfortable situations. (Acts 26:18) It's interesting working with the public--the world. It's so easy to get irritated with those who don't know Jesus; this can even be self-proclaimed Christians, and how their actions frustrate us in their response to situations and how they treat people. To those of us who know Jesus, and walk with Jesus, and reflect Him, and have been made new in Him, we have a hard time wrapping our head around how the world continues to live, and we forget that we too were once among the lost, dark and unpeaceful world. Grace. It's what saved us. In that moment when we died and received new life, we no longer hold on to this world or identify in what it offers. However, I don't think God wants us to lose touch with the world. After all, didn't He humble Himself taking off His crown? *"For God so loved the World that He gave the world Jesus, His son."* (John 3:16) Amazing love and grace, He met us, and loved us where we were. So we, too, must be like Christ in this way. To remember we once were lost, wretched, blind, wandering fools, hopeless with no peace, with everything dependent on what happened in the world, not knowing love, not embracing the true ways of the Lord. But now we know Him, so our speech can be full of compassion and grace toward those that are seeking Him; let our demeanor be praise worthy to the hope of His glory.

When people experience the frailty of this brokenness we live in, we must remember grace. That's all these people have to hang their life on. Remember to extend Christ and to show them somehow, some way that this isn't all there is. That's uncomfortable; it's messy. But if we live by His truths and know that because our treasure is laid up in Heaven, our hope is built on nothing less than Jesus' blood and righteousness. What He places in my hands here in this world is only by His grace. And what He will give me in the world to come, will too be because of grace.

I'm constantly asking God, "what's next?" My ears stay attuned to His voice and leadership, so desperately wanting to follow Him in all He has for me. I beg Him to use me and send me to do great things for His kingdom. I say this with a laugh because I often ask Him why I can't be a part of this or that, or be like this person or that person. Gently, He takes my hand and simply says, "Follow me. I'm protecting you, child." And with a sigh and a little disappointment, I follow Him, my face downcast until He shows me where He's taking me. Jesus loves me; this I know. He leads us places we never expect or even saw coming.

There is a cost to staying in our comfort zones. Are we dying in the settled life? One of Satan's strongholds is living a life of comfort. It is then that opportunities come along and we don't take them because we want to stay in our comfort zone. This is exactly where Satan wants you. I have equated it in my mind with hospice. Satan's goal is to keep us comfortable as we slowly die spiritually. Don't let him pump you up with things that temporarily numb your pain and temporarily comfort you. Don't be deceived; ever since Satan was thrown out of Heaven with a third of the angels, the agenda has been to prevent the exposing of Jesus. He will continue to do everything in his power to blind and deceive people. Again in John, Jesus warns that the enemy comes to "steal, kill, and destroy." He stops at nothing. Satan has no limits; he does not stop and consider that things might be too evil, too sinful, or too mean. He limits himself to nothing and uses all the resources and people that he can.

How do we combat that? God has no limits; He does not stop and consider that the things He commanded us to do might be too nice, or too loving, or too unconditional, or too truthful. We have the power of kingdom authority, and as children of God this is our mission. Before we step foot into another country to share Jesus, our feet must step across the street, and community, and city. This is the model in Acts 1:8. I've often wondered how it is possible to stay on the spiritual highs that we get on mission trips; then we come home and the "good feeling" wears off. Does it have to? The same very real God we encounter on mission trips can be encountered in our back yard. What is it that we do leading up to trips? Shouldn't we be expecting the same things for our community? Shouldn't we stay in a prepared state of mind and mission? The mission doesn't stop when we get home. Anything you want to be missional can be if it's done to the glory and mission of God. Throwing the

Frisbee, playing basketball, playing soccer with neighborhood kids, working at your job, cutting someone's grass...if you are showing people Christ's love and pouring His truth into their lives, then you are being missional.

My job became my mission field. I am learning that missions come in different forms. It's not always in the form of hammering nails and doing strenuous building projects. It's not always in the form of using words. God has used just simply used...me. The Gospel impacts our work in more ways than one. Not only are we called to do a good job in our work to the Glory of God, as if working for the Lord, but also the Gospel of our work is told in how we encounter and treat people. We can work really hard, but Jesus' Gospel, the good news of life, is for people. No amount of hard work we do will really matter unless we are allowing Christ in us to draw people to Himself by the deeds we do with our hands, by the words we speak with our lips, and by the love we extend with our hearts.

A young man came into the shop one day with large letters across his shirt reading, "ATHEIST." All my heart could do was love Him, and all I could pray was, "Jesus, help me show him through You in me that you are real and love him so much." My heart could not judge him; my heart didn't want to argue or prove him wrong. This compelled me all the more to serve him well and to show Him who Jesus is. It's the kindness of the Lord that leads to repentance. It isn't an "I'm better than you" attitude. It isn't an "I'll pray for you" attitude. I'm no better than the atheist. And if I were to really sit down and look at my life we could come to think that I must not really believe there is a God based on the way I don't trust Him in certain areas of my life. Lord, help my unbelief. The only way the atheist will ever come to know Jesus is by encountering a very real God in our lives. We don't have to know all the big scientific answers all the time. Customers at the shop noticed my smile most; they commented on how I smile all the time. After all Jesus has done in my life, how He has radically redefined and saved my life, how can I not smile? He's my reason to smile. He's my reason to do a good job at work. He's my reason for loving others. I pray He will always be revealed in our lives; He's so worthy of it. Did that young man know He encountered Jesus today? I pray we live lives worthy of the cross and the work that was accomplished on it. I pray we shout more with our lives than with our mouths that Jesus is alive! I pray we don't forget that God is always at work.

There is a verse that is used a lot when churches and missional organizations try to get people to answer the call to missions. It's found in Luke 10:2: "He told them, "The harvest is plentiful, but the workers are few. Ask the Lord of the harvest, therefore, to send out workers into his harvest field." While there may be some places where this verse can apply, what about the places where there isn't even a sign of a harvest? What happens when the field isn't ripe? When the field is still full of thorns and rocks, and there has been little cultivating or preparation done. I'll never forget a few years ago when I was on a mission trip in Dallas, Texas. We were on the Wycliffe campus doing some work, and I was assigned the task of clearing a field of big boulders and rocks. In the heat of July in Texas, that was A LOT of work. I'm pretty sure I sweat through my shirt twice and then some; I probably lost twenty pounds just through sweating. I'm exaggerating, but you get the point. This is a part of the work that must be done before there is a harvest. Pray for more workers who will prepare the soil. Think about the things that must happen before there can be a good harvest of crops. First, someone has to go and prepare the land, removing tree stumps, extracting rocks and moving them aside. I will never forget the verse God gave me on the plane when I flew back to my mission field of Portland, Oregon in August 2013. Joshua 1:3 says, "I am giving you what I promised Moses: Everywhere you go, you will be on land I have given you." I think this is key too. Our work is useless unless God gives us the land. We can work land all we want, but if God isn't in it...good luck. I have held tightly to this verse in the face of many discouragements and failures. After removing all the massive stuff, the soil has to be broken up, plowed, fertilized, and formed in orderly rows to prepare for the seed. The seeds then must be carefully planted and covered. But there is still no harvest. Maybe, like Nehemiah, we need to build a wall around our Jerusalem and protect what God has given. The seeds must be watered, nurtured, and fed. But then setbacks might occur: bad weather, insects...etc. However, even so, if attended to faithfully by the grace of God, a harvest will come.

CHAPTER SIX

Blessed Assurance

"For I am persuaded, that neither death, nor life, nor angels, nor principalities, nor powers, nor things present, nor things to come, Nor height, nor depth, nor any other creature, shall be able to separate us from the love of God, which is in Christ Jesus our Lord."

~Romans 8:38-39

As I flew over Portland and circled around this city, I prayed so fervently for the hearts of the people to open up and see their Creator God in the beauty that surrounds them. I love Portland. Jesus loves Portland, and His love is breaking through there. God is at work; I've had to ask Him over and over to give me fresh eyes to see Him work in a way I've never seen Him work before. It's been so powerful. God is not confined to our box or to how we think we know Him. Every city I've been to as a missionary, I leave knowing this is true, greater things are still to be done in this city that is the Lord's. I am convinced of this truth: God is making all things new. We were never created to go back to the old.

The church where I served, the pastor and his wife took a group of us to Multnomah Falls. It is so beautiful! I was reminded just how awesome our Creator is, not just in the vastness, power, and beauty of the waterfall, but in every tiny detail. The tiniest flower is as important as the waterfall. Not only that, but the truth that God created one little tiny flower for just me to see and notice brought me fresh eyes. We hiked up the mountain to the top of the falls; it was a mile up and so steep! Hiking up this steep narrow road, I couldn't help but think of what Jesus said in the gospel of Matthew. We walk a narrow road, and few ever find it. It's interesting because as we began our hike, the path was clogged with so many people. The higher you climb, though, the steeper and narrower it gets, and the fewer people you see. Oh, but what our eyes beheld when we made it to the top.

I have found in my walk with Jesus that He has me focus in on a particular word or topic and He will keep me there and teach me. Lately, He has been teaching me about the mystery of Himself and how to trust Him even when I don't fully know what's going on. Not only is there a mystery to God and His power, but there is a mystery in our limiting power. God desires to pour out blessing in our lives even in deep fiery trials. Psalm 78:41 states that the children of Israel limited the Holy One. "Limited" in Hebrew means "horizon." "This is as far we can see. This is all we can see that God can do." I have prayed the Prayer of Jabez since I was thirteen, that my horizons would be expanded, sometimes praying in the context of land and places. But now, I am praying in the context that God would expand the horizon of my belief and faith in Him--to see beyond what my eyes think they see and to believe God's limitless power because beyond the horizon is the promise.

What are some of the things that give us a "horizon" view? What is it in our lives that causes God's hands to be tied and unable to give the good He so desires to give? An unwilling spirit, refusing His invitation to Salvation, not wanting any more of God, an unclean lifestyle, harboring sin...these are all things that are easily fixed in and through Christ by repentance. When we look at the horizon on the ocean, we know that there is something more beyond what we see. There is more ocean and more land. I don't know about you, but I'm thankful to be in the hands of the Creator. I wish we could fully comprehend how precious we are to

Him, that He is for us, and that He wants to bless the life He has given to us.

Faith expects God to do great things, it's a life of anticipation of what He is going to do next. Sometimes it's exciting, and sometimes we are scared because we know these are moments that will either make us or break us. I don't know about you, but, I want to see the Lord do great wonders among us not just on Sunday, but every day.

Our faith is what shields us and gives us the strength to keep going. The more mountains we climb from the bottom of the valley, the stronger we become in trusting Jesus and sharing our faith with others. Such endurance brings us new perspective; we develop right responses and speak truth. It's so easy to quit, to give up, to burn out. This is where I found myself, fumbling with emotions, words, and thoughts; I sat at the table with a pencil that I wished could write what was so heavy on my heart. Questions filled my mind. Am I saying "no" to the flame that is molding and refining me? Dare my pen write these frights as thankfulness? But it does. That is the right response. I can do it because Christ is my strength, and He has equipped me for this mission. I began to write His promises, truths, and prayers. I cried out, I sought Him in His

Word. Why am I here? Am I failing? Do I have to keep fighting? The Lord stops me in Chapter Eight of the second book of Corinthians. In the Message it reads this:

"...so that what was so well begun could be finished up. You do so well in so many things—you trust God, you're articulate, you're insightful, you're passionate, you love us—now, do your best in this, too. I'm not trying to order you around against your will. But by bringing in the Macedonians' enthusiasm as a stimulus to your love, I am hoping to bring the best out of you. You are familiar with the generosity of our Master, Jesus Christ. Rich as he was, he gave it all away for us—in one stroke he became poor and we became rich. So here's what I think: The best thing you can do right now is to finish what you started last year and not let those good intentions grow stale. Your heart's been in the right place all along. You've got what it takes to finish it up, so go to it. Once the commitment is clear, you do what you can, not what you can't. The heart regulates the hands. This isn't so others can take it easy while you sweat it out. No, you're shoulder to shoulder with them all the way, your surplus matching their deficit, their surplus matching your deficit. In the end you come out even. As it is *written,*

Nothing left over to the one with the most

Nothing lacking to the one with the least."

This became a moment of repentance for me. The mission had to be completed when He said it was complete.

God broke me in Portland; it was anguish. But I walked away knowing this: if he gives me His burden, He will give me peace; if He breaks me, He will heal me. I found much hope to press on in the book of Nehemiah. All through the book, Nehemiah asks God to strengthen his hands to do His work. It reveals the result of his brokenness. The joy of the Lord is our strength! It's not a joy to remove pain, but to bear it; it is taking on the heart of God. It is only in the times where our faith meets testing and brokenness that we grow and He begins to do what He wants with us. I had nothing but God to rely on in Portland; He broke me from everything I could lean on. Everything was unexpected and unplanned; hard things happened. But it doesn't end with breaking. He makes it beautiful. He said, "I've broken you, but let me show you who I am and who you are." We are broken yet glorified. His body was broken for us; He rose up out of the grave alive. He doesn't leave us broken.

Our faith in Jesus tells His story through our lives. Obedience leads to a growing faith as we experience God. We have fear because we haven't learned to trust Him; we haven't really experienced His hand of unending love and amazing grace, the deep love that flows from Christ to work miracles in our lives. If you think about the stories and prophecies proclaimed in the Bible, they are all centered on an action the individual experienced from God Himself. This brings us into unity with God our Father, Jesus our Savior, and the Holy Spirit our guide.

Thousands of feet in the air flying into Chicago from Portland, I looked down on the Earth, and the wonder of getting to meet with the Creator was astounding. I was so tired; my body felt dead, but the Spirit inside of me was alive! I had my Bible open to John 17, where Jesus is praying for all who are His. How does the world believe God sent His Son Jesus? Jesus never took glory or accolades unto Himself, but always pointed His power back to His Father, God in Heaven. This is a powerful thought! Being one with Him means everything! He created the world, and loves the world, and will enable those bound to Him to reach the world effectively for Him. BE THIS!!

When God shows up radically, it's really hard to be quiet. The power is the Holy Spirit in us. In John's letters to the seven churches, he uses the phrase, "listen to what the Spirit is saying." He may lead us to say something so simple to someone whose heart He has been working in and drawing to Himself; it will be just what they need to hear. Suddenly, what seems so simple becomes profound. When we prayerfully enter a room and discern the Spirit's voice by asking Him to show us where He is working, He will reveal it. When we ask Him what needs to be heard, He will give us the words to speak and pray. What is leading someone to Christ apart from Christ? God's voice cannot be heard until we silence our own. Truth will never be heard as long as we are shouting our opinions just to be right. My pastor said something so profound several years ago, it has stuck with me ever since. He was preaching from 1 Peter 3 in the context of husbands and wives. So many times as women we have the innate nature to just speak our mind and let whatever fly out of our mouth when we are upset. My pastor said, "We should never be known as women who speak our mind, but as women who speak Christ's mind and truth."

One particular Easter at my church, I was serving on the altar counseling ministry. The night before, I had prepared, gone over all the theological and doctrinal systems; I had written out the story of redemption from creation to the new Heaven and earth. My Scriptures were ready. So the end of the service came, and was I ever ready to see what God was going to do and who He would allow me to lead to Him. Preacher motioned for me to come over; I grabbed up my Bible, and there stood a little 5 year old boy. Preacher looked at me and said, "He wants to pray to receive Jesus, can you take him back and walk him through and pray with him?" Oh my. Now you have to know I was afraid of children in this season of my life; we were not on the same level. God made me level that day. Out the window went everything I came prepared with, and in that moment God humbled me as I had to quiet my heart to hear His Spirit speak using simple words and a calm loving voice. Jesus and His Good News is so simple because the Gospel is for everyone. In fact, Jesus told us to have faith like the little children!! Even if we have faith as small as a mustard seed, faith is faith, and when it's in Him every bit matters and counts. Do you believe? We don't stand alone in battle. There is nothing separating us from Him or each other. Fresh eyes of faith, that's what we need, and we won't have to be afraid because we'll be persuaded, and will have seen with our own eyes His glory.

CHAPTER SEVEN

What Must I Do?

"Ah, Sovereign Lord, you have made the heavens and the earth by your

great power and outstretched arm. Nothing is too hard for you."

Jeremiah 32:17

When we read the Bible, we'll come to parts where the Pharisees mock Jesus, how people treat those who are diseased, the man who insulted Jesus on the cross. I like to think I'd be just like Jesus, at least like Peter. After all there is no way we could be like those unfair Pharisee's, or like the people who do things that is not Christ like. We're good people. Some of us believe this *good* gets us into Heaven and makes God accept, and love us more. But the more I humble myself and truly let God reveal to me who I am in the mirror of His Word, the more I see that I am the Pharisee, I am the one who treats the diseased badly, and I insult Jesus on a constant basis.

In Luke 23 Jesus is having a conversation with the two men hanging on either side of Him on the cross.

"One of the criminals who hung there hurled insults at him: "Aren't you the Messiah? Save yourself and us!" But the other criminal rebuked him. "Don't you fear God," he said, "since you are under the same sentence? We are punished justly, for we are getting what our deeds deserve. But this man has done nothing wrong."

The thought came to me, what a picture of the grace God is extending to us. He's showing us a picture of who we are, and who we can be using the example of these men. There are times when we encounter circumstances in our lives that seem to nearly crucify us. We shake our fist at God and insult Him shouting, "Aren't you God?! Do something about this! If you were God you would save me from this!" There are sayings out there and some people who say it's okay to do this to Jesus. I don't think it is to be quite honest. The other criminal said the correct thing, he feared God. He saw the sin in his own life, and realized the death he was dying was just, but something in him pushed him to asked Jesus to remember him. Jesus did something shocking, he pushed up on the nails that held Him there and extended grace to this bad criminal. We never do know what his crime is: rape, murder, all we know is it was pretty bad to call for crucifixion. It was and probably still is in some countries the most shameful, and painful form of execution. It took days for some to die on the cross.

This grace extended from Jesus made the Pharisee's furious. Heaven was reserved for them after all, they kept all the commandments, they were drowning in their own righteousness and had faith in themselves. But Jesus didn't come to set up a new order where the good guys keep winning. He became the friend of sinners. The ones who had no hope, or even a chance of someone looking their way.

No matter how bad you think you are, or how good you think you are for that matter, you aren't beyond the reach of God's grace. Receive, and be clothed in His righteousness. Good people don't go to Heaven, bad people don't go to Heaven...Forgiven people do by the way of the cross. People who humble themselves before Jesus and say, *"God I fear you, I am your servant, I admit I'm a sinner, I see it in my life, and that I deserve death! But Jesus you are here, next to me, you died with my sin on you. God if you would just remember me; if you would just think of me I have the faith to know you can and will save me."*

Jesus invited everyone to be saved, and everyone gets in the same way, and is able to meet the requirement according John 3:16

"For God so loved the world (everyone), that He gave His everlasting Son (Jesus) and whosoever (everyone) believes (requirement) in Him (Jesus) will have eternal life." The criminal believed. The question is do you? Not did you pray this prayer one time. Have you seen the sin that is poison and applied the blood to your life? It's getting a DNA change, it's a new life, another chance with Jesus' blood running through your veins.

After one of my return visits home I had the honor of addressing the choir I sang in at my church and sharing the mission work God had been letting me do in Portland. Later that night a good friend of mine e-mailed me and told me something God revealed to her driving home after hearing me speak. This is what her email said to me:

I don't want to put words in God's mouth, but He may have shown me something. I was praying as I got home and I think He may have given this to me...Pray for a rich man in Portland to be saved....this verse came immediately... "Again I say to you, it is easier for a camel to go through the eye of a needle, than for a rich man to enter the kingdom of God."

This moved me so deeply, since that email I have prayed so fervently everyday for the rich man in Portland to be saved. I also have studied and read the story of the Rich Young Ruler from Mark 10:17-31. There is so much depth in this story, so much to see and be aware of especially in the sense of coming to Jesus. The rich ruler came and threw himself at Jesus' feet and exclaimed, "Good teacher, what do I do to inherit eternal life?" Immediately Jesus stops him in his flattery towards him. He tells the ruler first, not call Him good and directs Him toward God saying that only God is good. We see Jesus doing this all the time throughout scripture, Jesus was the Messiah(teacher), we shouldn't cling to our teachers, or see that our teachers/pastors/leaders can save us, only God is good, Salvation only comes through God the Father. There is a question that must be asked when we put works in the mix with Salvation, and that is, "How good is good enough?" Weather you keep the commandments or not, no one is good but God.

In the next part, I love that Jesus looked at Him and loved him...He loved him while in his sin! That's the Good News Paul writes of in Romans, "while we were still yet sinners, Christ died for us." Yet, he also loved us enough to not leave us in our sin. Jesus challenged the young man in the way of how bad did he want to have eternal life? Was it enough to give everything away? Do you see what Jesus was continuously doing? He was aiming for all this mans idols: being good, and money namely. You see, we all want goodness, but so few want it enough to pay the price. We see throughout the Gospels over and over how Jesus demolished the Jewish standard. In this story the Jews saw that if a man was prosperous, he was a good, moral man and he must have had the favor of God. But in the end money can't save you, neither can your good works, nor all the power this man possessed. So, who can be saved?

If salvation depended on a mans own effort it would be impossible for everyone. But Salvation is a gift from God, and all things are possible to Him. Jeremiah exclaims in his book, "Ah, Sovereign Lord, you have made the heavens and the earth by your great power and outstretched arm. Nothing is too hard for you." (32:17) There is no one God can't save, but there are times that we put our own limits on God. When we continually reject Him. This young man did, and Jesus didn't run after him either! He watched him walk away then turned to his disciples, the ones who had done the very thing Jesus asked this young man. Who are you trusting? Things or God?

There is another neat aspect of this story. It is the promise Jesus gives all those who will follow Him for the sake of the Gospel. Though we might leave behind family, or have to forsake family, Jesus is pointing to a Father in heaven. Even earlier in this passage of scripture Jesus calls his disciples, "Children." That's what we are...we who have accepted the Father's love. The Greek term "*agapetos*" is used 61 times from the book of Matthew to the book Jude in the Bible. It means beloved, that we personally experience God's agape love. We see a great picture of what it means to be a child of God in 1 John 2:28-3:3. John is encouraging the child of God to continue in Him who saved him. This is the reason and order of the Christian life. If we continue in Him; if we abide in Him...there must have been a beginning. As the sweet old hymn goes, "the hour I first believed." When we live like Jesus, we do Jesus stuff, and that is what Jesus was stressing to the Rich Young Ruler. You want eternal life? Sell everything you have, take up your cross because we are not only in Christ through the resurrection, but also in the death of Christ. We are maturing into a selfless believer; it is the act of becoming humble. That's what Mark outlines as Jesus being like, a servant. He's calling us to do the same. The Gospel is not "do the right thing because it's the right thing to do." There is another facet missing. If we want to continue to be in Him, we must see.... "I once was blind but now I see." Either we are a child of God or we aren't. If we are we must, "Therefore bear fruits worthy of repentance..." -Luke 3:8

John was preparing the way for Jesus, showing people that they need a Savior to save them from the law that they can't keep. We read in the Gospels that he was going throughout all the region around Jordan preaching a baptism of repentance for the remission of sins. In this, there are two important Greek words to know:

hamartia- 'sin': (n) any action or attitude that is contrary to the will of God, and the revealed standard of God.

metanoia- 'repented': (n) changing from a sinful state to a righteous standard. Not merely regret, but a change of perspective that results in changed actions.

In John's preaching we see the High Priests, Sadducee's and the Pharisee's, tax collectors, and soldiers come along and ask what they must do. John, though calling them a brood of vipers, still answers their question and in the same way Jesus did the Rich Young Ruler, "Let him who has give to those who have not." In other words get rid of your idols and gods. Give your life away, and find it. The high teachers prided themselves on the law and knowing scripture but in that moment John shows them that they had broken a commandment, and not from the 10 Commandments so much as the greatest one of all, to love your neighbor has yourself. The next "what shall we do" comes from the tax collectors, John answers saying, don't steal, again pointing to the 10 Commandments and their lack of keeping it. Next, the soldiers ask, and again John says, don't steal, don't covet, and don't lie about people.

One of the many things these "brood of snakes" prided themselves on was their kinship and being in the line of Abraham. They would walk around saying, "Abraham is our Father." They thought since that was the case it would be enough to get them into Paradise. However, as we touched on a little bit ago, Christianity is about God being our Father. We can't merely cling to our teachers and who we think as being our father, forefathers, and think that's good enough to save us. Abraham is not savior, nor is he the high priest pleading on our behalf to God the Father. John came back at them saying, it doesn't matter who is in your tree if you are living apart from God. He'll cut you off and throw you in the fire. This is pointing to the parable of the vine and branches. He then talks about the chaff and and wheat and talks about God separating and throwing in the fire that which is not worth keeping around. The vineyard and the chaff is open ended. Will you repent? It is by your own confession, belief, and repentance, not Abraham's, and not the fact that you are learned in the Bible. "This is to my Fathers glory, that you bear much fruit showing yourself to be my disciples." -John 15:8

I was presented with the question "How do we begin to penetrate the Spiritual Darkness that surrounds us, and do it effectively?" John 15 says simply by abiding in Christ. The book of John is my favorite Gospel. It's deeply theological, and one of the main themes is believing. The word *believe* is used close to 88 times. The Greek word for believe is *pisteuo*, and means to put ones faith in; to trust. [John 6:22-58] My heart leaps and is so overwhelmed for the truth that comes from this and how beautiful Jesus is. I pray you can feel my emotion leaping off these pages as you read, and grasp the intimacy of not only my love for you, but Christ's love for you, and the relationship He so desires to have with you. Please don't miss the depth of this.

First and foremost we see a beautiful picture in verse one alone. It is the picture of the vineyard. In particular this is pointing to Isaiah 5 and 27. In Chapter 5 of Isaiah it is the Song of the Vineyard which expresses God's accusation of the wicked leadership that had ruined his vineyard, Israel. There then is a transformation over in chapter 27 the Redemption pointing to Jesus. It is the Father restoring. In the 23rd Psalm we know that he restores our soul. When we restore something, or put a lot of work into something like a garden or a sports car, we say, "Yeah, my blood, sweat, and tears when into it." When we stop a moment and consider this statement against the Father as our Gardener, and consider what Jesus did for us on the cross. Literally, blood, sweat, and tears goes into making us the children we ought of to be of God. I think that same saying can be said of believers at times. Abiding in Christ is no easy task, when we abide we endure, believe, we wait, accept, dwell, trust, and rest. It affects every part of our life and our individual ministries for the Kingdom of God. We abide through prayer, by faith, and in reading His

Word. Reading His Word is what prunes us, the Greek for prunes means "he cleans." When we read our Bible and receive the truth and apply it we are allowing God to cleanse us and wash away sin that may be brewing in our mind or heart. John tells us in his first chapter that Jesus is the Word. He makes me clean, through His blood I am clean.

Another way we remain in Christ is through relationships. God as our gardener is such a picture. If we were to go back to the 23rd Psalm, we see that He makes us lie down in green pastures. Green pastures don't just happen, it takes a lot of time and cultivating of the soil to make a pasture green and lush. So it is when we prunes...when He cuts away at things that don't need to be there so we can be healthy. The whole idea behind abiding in Christ is our complete dependency in Him. Jesus says very clearly a branch that is apart from me dies and is thrown out in the burn pile. Apart from Jesus we don't survive. Apart from each other we don't survive either. There are three categories of people that Jesus had a relationship with, who He was investing in: The Father, His disciples/other believers, and the lost. Our relationships should look that this as well. Without these relationships we become ineffective, and are no longer abiding in Christ the way we should be. All of them require us to be in tune with Him. Of course at the base of every relationship is love. Love is laying our lives down for the sake of another. Whatever makes up our life and we give it to another sacrificially, that is laying our lives down for them, love.

When we do all of these things Jesus tells us to ask whatever we wish and it will be done for you. Many take this verse out of context and do not consider it's full meaning or even take into consideration that it's not all about them, but all about Jesus. You see, when all of who we are abides in Christ, what we want no longer matters. We are no more concerned about the other, and building the Kingdom. I do not mean that God will not give us what we need. That's the difference. We will depend on Him more for what our real needs are rather than the nice new "under the sun" things the World convinces us that we need. Abiding in Christ is above the sun living. It empowers us to live for something more than ourselves and trying to do life on our own.

The Vine you gotta see is Jesus, He is the true vine. [John 15:1] His vines are totally worth following, and being apart of. It's the life source, Jesus is saying, "Whatever you need, I AM..." But in order to experience Him we have to be apart of who He is.

In the book of John predominately, Jesus reveals Himself in "I AM" statements. In this Jesus pulls the curtain back on His true identity and ministry. He purposefully used "I AM" to reference the Old Testament and show Himself as the same God who gave manna from Heaven as being also:

The Messiah (4:26)

The Light of the World (8:12)

The Bread of Life (6:35)

The gate for the sheep (10:7-9)

The Good Shepherd (10:11-14)

The Resurrection and the Life (11:25)

The Way,Truth,and Life (14:6)

The Vine (15:1-5)

He didn't reveal Himself as I AM to only Moses, He is still revealing Himself that way today in my life and yours. He is.

Many times we pursue Christianity and Jesus for what we can gain. We claim verses where Jesus says "ask whatever you will and I'll do it." However, how quickly we look over what the surrounding verses say.

Only when our prayers are controlled by His Word will He give. Only when our hearts line up with His truth, and we realize it's not about what we gain, but what He pours through us. We don't get to keep for ourselves selfishly what God blesses us with. God's purposes are not merely to make us beautiful plump grapes, but to squeeze the sweetness out of us and thus the lives we come in contact with will be continually refreshed. Sometimes that squeezing is painful. Being fruitful isn't about a show or how beautiful we are. It's all about others, and the glory of Jesus. Our spiritual lives are measured by what the world deems as successful, but only by what God pours through us. This cannot be measured. Only in Him is there life, and in that life is the pouring out He wants to give to help us grow and stay strong, but we have to stay attached.

There is a beautiful promise to this passage of scripture: The comforter/Spirit of Truth remains in me. The genuine follower of Christ never experiences the condition of not having the abiding Spirit of God. Not for one moment will He forsake, or walk away.

PART THREE:

I STAND FIRM...

THE GIFT OF TRUTH

CHAPTER EIGHT

In Freedom

"You will know the truth and the truth will set you free."

John 8:32

The truth sets us free, not so we can do whatever we want, nor so we can agree with whatever we want. If it doesn't line up with the Bible, don't do it! Following Christ means doing what God wants. God wants us to accept His son, Jesus, and stop doing what is wrong whether we think it's wrong or not. We're right back to repentance, which is agreeing with God that what we did was wrong, and turning from it. J.I. Packer said, "Anytime we don't practice repentance of our sins, and preach repentance for others sins, we're heretics." Turning away from sin and turning to truth is essential. It is our fruit that determines false and truth in our lives. John says in His Gospel (8:32), "You will know the truth, and the truth will set you free." A couple of verses earlier, Jesus identifies His

Father as being truth (v.26), and then Jesus identifies Himself as the truth.

Jesus is teaching the Pharisees. In the beginning of John 8, they brought a prostitute before Jesus, saying she should die for her sin by being stoned. Do you know what Jesus invited her to do after her accusers left? He invited her to turn from her sin through repentance and the desire to not sin anymore. The Pharisees then declared war on God. This is where we all fall. The issue ceases to be about the sinner, but about God; the accusations are no longer about what the woman did, but about what Jesus didn't do, and what He said. Jesus starts rebuking the Pharisees for not believing, saying, "You are of this world, I am not. Unless you believe you will die in your sins." Do you see what Jesus is extending to them? An invitation to repentance and change, but The Pharisees were much too caught up in culture applauding them. We too face this. Would we rather have culture applauding and Jesus rebuking, or Jesus applauding and culture rebuking?

In Verse 31, Jesus says, "You are truly my disciples IF you keep obeying my teachings." This means we must keep walking in truth, not walking in sin, not agreeing with sin, and not tolerating sin. We must have Jesus applauding and culture rebuking. That is knowing the Father, and the

Father setting you free (v.32). Jesus addresses again that one must choose who his master is. They answered "Abraham." I think the choices were "God" or "Satan." There is no such thing as a half-lie, or a half-truth. Satan is a liar (v.44); Jesus is the truth. (John 18:37-38, Isaiah 45:19)

So what do you believe? This is why doctrine and theology matter!! Because it's not so much how we behave, but how we believe, for that belief which will be rooted in our hearts will determine how we behave. Loving is good, and serving is good, but knowing what you believe is even better. Real love tells the truth, and how can you tell the truth if you do not know it? Has the truth set you free? Shoseki, a philosopher once said, "Truth only reveals itself when one gives up all preconceived ideas." This sums up the danger of religion, tradition and pride. Religion is a corruption of the gospel. Tradition is fear of change. Pride is the root of most every sin. All these things can make me incapable of receiving and perceiving the truth. May I humble myself continually, acknowledging my infinite limitation and my finite understanding so that I may receive truth and therefore grow in Christ.

There are times we have to affirm out loud and stand firm in our position, to refuse to be moved off the promises of God. I'm pretty good at standing firm in what I believe. His Word is truth, and a lot of time we need a truth encounter more than we do power, or zen-like sayings, or whatever floats around Facebook. This is true for me too. We must always come back to truth. What I have learned about freedom is this: we are as free as we allow ourselves to be. Why be free? Well, why not?! The Lord took me back to Exodus, where the Hebrew people were enslaved. God was going to set them free through Moses. The truth of this story and their freeing is that God didn't free the children of Israel so that they could relax poolside and drink sweet tea for the rest of their lives. God set them free so that they could fulfill their mission – to become a "light to the nations" (Isaiah 51:4). Just as Jesus fulfilled all the prophecies about Him, God has written our stories, and there are things we still have yet to fulfill for Him! There is a mission, and many need to hear the gospel truth; we are called to be a light. Be free so God can use you to be a freeing agent in others people's lives.

If we do not repent, God will war against us! He wars with truth, scripture, and The Word of God (Ephesians 6, and Hebrews 4) which sometimes results in the destruction of nations. We must ALWAYS come back to the Word of God; it is our spiritual victory! We must speak the truth, because the truth is being suppressed in unrighteousness (Romans 1). What we are seeing in our culture today more than ever before is people trading the truth for a lie. Deep inside of us we know what the truth is; it is instinctive to us. It's not a matter of acceptance that holds people back from admitting their sin or the lifestyle they have chosen, it's that innate conviction from God that is yelling, "THIS IS WRONG!" Romans 1:18 says that God shows his anger to those who push His truth away from them. That's what some of the churches, and even some churches today embrace, forming a version of Christianity that doesn't command repentance, but tolerates and affirms sin. Jesus rebuked these churches because they have denied His plan for creation and design for how humans should function. All lifestyles are not acceptable! However, it's not unforgivable. This is what we miss. There is hope! Jesus didn't leave us hopeless in our sin. He is the one who sets us free. Jesus' love is not necessarily tolerance, but is instead inviting everyone who believes in Him (John 3:16) to come to the foot of the cross and die with Him! And instead of trading the truth for a lie, doing what Martin Luther called "The Great Exchange." 2 Corinthians 5:17-21:

17 This means that anyone who belongs to Christ has become a new person. The old life is gone; a new life has begun! 18 And all of this is a gift from God, who brought us back to himself through Christ. And God has given us this task of reconciling people to him. 19 For God was in Christ, reconciling the world to himself, no longer counting people's sins against them. And he gave us this wonderful message of reconciliation. 20 So we are Christ's ambassadors; God is making his appeal through us. We speak for Christ when we plead, "Come back to God!" 21 For God made Christ, who never sinned, to be the offering for our sin, so that we could be made right with God through Christ.

CHAPTER NINE

Faithfully and Lovingly

"All these faithful ones died without receiving what God had promised them, but they saw it all from a distance and welcomed the promises of God..." ~Hebrews 11:13

One Sunday night, I sat and confessed some things to my Spiritual Mother in the Lord and asked her how I keep missing when Satan attacks? What in my mind needs to change and think differently in that regard? I didn't understand why I couldn't automatically detect that it was Satan throwing his hate my way. I have unrealistic expectations of wanting to know when and how quickly I can get out of battle and have Satan leave me alone. It's not that we let him attack us purposefully, or aren't ready, but a lot of war depends on whether or not we are afraid. That's the first "uh-oh": giving into fear. I think we have been deluded into thinking that warfare is a quick-step methodical process. But it's not; it's messy. I was in all the right places that day, at church, in the Word, singing to the Lord, praying, trying to lay this burden at the altar; I reached out for help. We can have a plan; we can resolve not to be afraid and not let fear take over our lives. But I still think at the end of the day the war is won by not giving up and by just being faithful. We might get hit on all sides, but what's important is to keep going; get right back up and into the game. Even more, it is realizing that we need people to stand with us, if you are an introvert like me, this in itself is scary. We like to be in our room alone, and we certainly don't want to ruin anyone's day by telling them we need some help getting out of the chokehold Satan has us in.

Most every day I am faced with a temptation. I share this story because God is really teaching me that He can be trusted and that He is faithful, and I have opportunity to glorify Him in my actions. I was feeling really bad when I started to get sick. I had a major headache; I was tired and not thinking straight. I had gone to Target to get some medicine and all of a sudden out of nowhere Satan attacked! Spiritual battle was engaged; immediately I resisted the temptation and walked away. Scripture reminds me that Jesus gets temptation and doesn't leave us without a way out. He is so faithful. In resisting Satan, Jesus got the glory.

That's been really powerful for me to experience. He gave me a way out. The difference is that I took it.

James 1:12-18 explains the power when we overcome temptation:

*12 Blessed is the man who endures temptation; for when he has been approved, he will receive the crown of life which the Lord has promised to those who love Him. 13 Let no one say when he is tempted, "I am tempted by God"; for God cannot be tempted by evil, nor does He Himself tempt anyone. 14 But each one is tempted when he is drawn away by his own desires and enticed. 15 Then, when desire has conceived, it gives birth to sin; and sin, when it is full-grown, brings forth death. 16 Do not be deceived, my beloved brethren. 17 Every good gift and every perfect gift is from above, and comes down from the Father of lights, with whom there is no variation or **shadow of turning**. 18 Of His own will He brought us forth by the word of truth, that we might be a kind of firstfruits of His creatures.*

I love how it says in Verse Seventeen that there is "no shadow of turning." It took me back to the old hymn, "Great is the Thy Faithfulness." This hymn has always been dear to my heart: *Great is thy faithfulness oh God my Father, there is no shadow of turning with thee. Thou changest not, thy compassions they fail not. As thou hast been, thou forever wilt be. Great is thy faithfulness!* It all starts with the simple act of acknowledging Him. Satan doesn't want us to take that way out. He doesn't want Jesus to be glorified or praised. Just as God is showing Himself faithful to us, this is our opportunity to be faithful to Him. This is how we reflect His glory. It's the glory of His grace, the grace to give us a way out. We are to make the most of all the Father gives us. It's His grace that gives me the strength to overcome. It's His grace that gives me another chance. It's His grace that allows these feeble hands to praise Him. I breathe in His grace and breathe out praise. To God be the glory, the One who does not let me slip or fall, who never sleeps and watches over me, who is with me, and guides my way. He is faithful. *Lord find me faithful in You.*

All of us will face trials and testing, and in those times our true character and beliefs come to light. We may be tempted to shake our fist at God, or we can pray and ask Him for wisdom (v.5). God will always hear His children and give us everything we need to take us through...not out, not over, not under, simply through. I read a neat quote not long ago that said this, "Sometimes I feel like I'm drowning in responsibilities, but I've experienced God's grace enough to know that if I did drown He would enable me to breathe underwater." Abiding in His grace. It's knowing we can ask Him for anything we need to get through the test and trial. He didn't put us on Earth and say 'Good Luck! I hope you manage well.' No!! He's given us countless gifts and tools, and will give us many more if we just ask. People want to throw grace around, when they've given into temptation, they write Grace over it and keep going in a downward spiral toward death, and this is never really what God intended. I don't think I really have the right to put definitions and stuff on things that are God's, but these are just my observations in life. The joy of trials is knowing that in the end it leads to Jesus, and that we are able to identify with our Savior. It's what produces fruit in our lives. Apart from Christ, it's depressing. The trial won't grow us, or better us, it will embitter us and suffocate life out of us.

Endure to the end, dear Christ follower. Keep following Christ in the face of everything God allows to pass through His hands to you. It's for a good reason. Let His Word continue to come alive in you. Don't follow the false teachings that try to make you feel good and trick you into thinking that life should be a flower and unicorn experience where you shouldn't be going through trials, and since you are you must have some kind of unconfessed sin or hidden hatred. That's not for another to point out. Stay in a tight relationship with Jesus. This life is what God gave you uniquely...don't waste it, don't throw it away. I love what a friend of mine says, "We're running a marathon, not a sprint." Sometimes I think we sprint through life and circumstances. We want it to be over quickly and hurry up and get through this. Endure, keep the pace, slow and steady wins the race; perseverance.

Spiritual warfare is refusing to move, to stay planted where God has us, to stay behind the cross and Christ's shed blood. We refuse to let Satan pass through and take one of our own. We protect each other, locking arms, and stand unified on the truths of God's Word. This takes courage and intentional initiative. Right away in Portland, I started to frequent a Starbucks close to where I was living at the time. I had prepared for Portland months before I went. I knew to a degree what to expect. I started to form relationships with people. I quickly learned that this is the only way to really earn a voice and trust in their life. They are all about authenticity. That's why relationships are so important. I went to Starbucks most every day and just had a presence there. Sometimes I was able to talk to people, but sometimes I just sat faithfully reading my Bible or playing on the computer. I took the initiative to do work outside the church walls and in the intern work I was assigned.

To anyone who shares the Gospel and puts forth the Word and truth, the most discouraging thing is to have no one accept Jesus. For the missionary to go home and report no salvations is as if to say, "I'm not being effective here. I'm not having an impact." I was reminded not long ago that God didn't send me to Portland to fix it. God doesn't send the missionary anywhere to fix anything; if He wanted to fix something, He would because He's the only real "fixer." Mission work isn't about us; it's not about getting a good feeling or getting to pat ourselves on the back for a job well done, or thinking we just changed the world. If you look in your rear view mirror as you leave a city, is it in better or worse shape? Maybe we cause more accidents than good?

So, what's the blessing of missionary work? It's in finding the lost and letting them know that they are wanted. I think what makes the angels lean over the rails as they watch us is not what big huge things we will do, but I believe they look for the small yet faithful things we will do.

Will we smile at this person? How will we react to this situation? And I believe they cheer when these small actions bring glory to the Father. Haven't we heard the stories of faithful missionaries who dedicated their whole lives in another country without seeing even one person embrace Jesus as Savior, only to learn that fifty years later there was a tremendous harvest? In our instant-gratification society, we would prefer to bypass the hard work and go directly to the harvest. How do we respond when the work goes more slowly than we would like to see? Andrew Murray wrote to this effect:

> *"Let no friend of missions become discouraged when the work proceeds slowly. Among our forefathers in Europe, a whole century was occupied with the introduction of Christianity. Sometimes a nation received Christianity to cast it off again after thirty or forty years. It required a thousand years to bring them up to where we now stand."*

It's hard to stand firm and be faithful when it doesn't even look like anything is happening. In fact, in this very day and time in our own nation, many of us are not standing firm or faithful in the ways of the Lord; we are not pointing people to the cross.

According to Pew Research Center, statistics show that Christianity is on the decline in America, and Non-Christian, and unaffiliated people are on the rise. One of the radio talk show hosts I've listened to for 27 years did a story on this research stating that "Christians still have power in this Country if they just used it." He went on further to say, "But even with this drop, 70% of the country still identifies as Christians, so how is it that less than one million people can influence a country when it comes to political issues? By the same token, how is it that 70% of the population can be bullied and silenced and coerced into accepting societal evolution with which they disagree because of their religious beliefs? It's not just the Republican Party caving. There's a whole lot of groups that make up the majority in this country one way or the other who are not pushing back."

The only way to be the true Church of Jesus Christ, those saved by His costly grace of sacrifice, is to remember just that. Jesus isn't like a band you follow; He can make you feel really good and sing along, but all good bands come to an end. We do not follow Jesus when we feel like it. Abiding in Him is a constant thing, not when it's convenient and accommodates our lifestyle. We follow and abide even when we face loss, severe suffering and persecution (especially then for the sake of Christ!), when our hearts ache, when we are poor and have little, and in times of testing.

Bonhoffer had it right when he compared grace to the sinner as either being cheap or costly in his book, "The Cost of Discipleship." No one can really stand firm on a cheap grace because it is a perversion of the Gospel and not truth. Cheap grace is being "religious" for an hour a week; it is the exaltation of grace itself, taking the place of Jesus. It is the lie that all behavior in life is covered by grace, and nothing changes inward or outward. But as the title of his book suggests, there is a cost involved in being a true disciple and follower of Christ. We know the truth, and believe in Jesus' death on the cross that gave us new life when we accepted Him as Lord. Continuous thankfulness pours out from our heart in that Jesus took our place because of our sin and set us free. (Colossians 2:6-15) We believe that our sin should have separated us forever from God, but because of His great love for us and in the new lives we now live, we set our minds and hearts on Jesus and acknowledge that He is the hope of glory. When truth is accepted, it requires daily obedience to the Holy Spirit in a changing behavior with citizenship affirmed in Heaven with Jesus.

So, how do we reconcile with, and impact a culture and generation who is dying to live and be loved, especially if cheap grace is the going rate? We can no longer manipulate and market the Gospel as "cheap." We can no longer lean on the preacher or those "better" church people. Our lives need to have a truth encounter; our heart and mouth must cry out to God in sorrow for not standing firm in what we believe. For sitting back and allowing Satan to take our kids out. For seeing ourselves as being better or having more blessings than another culture who doesn't know Jesus. The ministry of reconciliation is when what we proclaim with our mouths through evangelism is validated by how we live our life. We separate ourselves from moral wrong. Over and over Paul says, "STAND FIRM!" Don't move off the rock of Jesus. Don't let up your anchor in Him. Stand firm. Stand firm! Push back.

Many are drawn to Portland because of the beauty, and while it has been delightful to encounter my great God's creation, I see more beauty in the people. Their pierced faces, tattooed bodies, and colorful hair. Don't ask me why, but my heart fills with love when I lay eyes on these folks. They have a story to tell, and I wonder if I'm listening and loving well. I wonder many more things, like whether our hearts truly seek God and we don't even know it. Do the people surrounding me know the Creator of all of this like I know Him? Do they know there is a Creator? Do they know His name? Have they heard? Most of all, do they know how much more beautiful they are to Him than what their eyes behold? This is a truth God spoke over me not long ago. I have always been so taken with creation, and rightfully so. It is a part of special revelation, a gift God gave to reveal Himself. Often times, however, we get too caught up in what fills our eyes and not in the "Whom" behind it all. My breath was taken away on a clear day, revealing the majestic Mount Hood; I whispered, "Wow." Normally God lets me have my moment, but this time He spoke. He said, "You know you are as beautiful to me as Mt. Hood is to you. You take my breath away." WOW! Seriously. Most days I can hardly stand myself, and I take God's breath away, and you do too! You know why? Because we were made in His image. We are more valuable to Him than anything in this world. Do you know how precious you are to Jesus?

I went on a Spiritual retreat to Cannon Beach at the beginning of 2014, just needing to get away and regroup and ask God for a miracle. I've always connected with God in His creation, joining in with nature worshiping its maker. On this retreat, I was up into the late hours in His Word, writing out frustrations, examining myself and where I may be failing. In the wee hours of the morning, I found myself stretched out on the floor asleep in front of the fireplace. When I woke up, I went out on the patio area and looked out at the Pacific Ocean. After taking a long walk to the famous rock, I got back to my room and cozied up in front of the fireplace with my Bible and a little bit of breakfast. God led me to John 21, Breakfast by the Sea:

> "At dawn Jesus was standing on the beach, but the disciples couldn't see who he was. He called out, "Friends, have you caught any fish? Bring some of the fish you've just caught," Jesus said. So Simon Peter went aboard and dragged the net to the shore. There were 153 large fish, and yet the net hadn't torn. "Now come and have some breakfast!" Jesus said. None of the disciples dared to ask him, "Who are you?" They knew it was the Lord. Then Jesus served them the bread and the fish." John 21:4,10-14

Through this entire chapter, He showed Himself to me just as I needed to see Him. He showed Himself as my Father, Provider, Lord over creation, Friend, and Satisfier. He would keep me in this chapter for the remainder of my mission in Portland, teaching me so much about ministering to people and cultivating a community of grace. This cannot be done apart from Him; trust me I've tried, and it doesn't work.

There are so many aspects of this chapter that have absolutely challenged, pushed, blessed, and convicted me. I think I could write a book alone on John 21......oh wait......I am writing a book! But I would advise you, before you go and read John 21 for yourself asking God to change you, to be ready for change because He will bring it to you, and you will be uncomfortable and wish you had never gone there. This is a chapter about nurturing and protecting Christ's followers; it's a chapter of faith and commitment. It's about stepping into a leadership role and answering the call to be an example. It means being prepared so those whom you are guiding will have something. The responsibility of stewardship in loving and caring for those that Jesus calls His. I love how

Jesus takes ownership; they aren't my sheep, they aren't Peter's sheep, they're God's.

For this book though, Jesus is the focus, because He teaches us how to serve and what we as the body should be known for. Jesus' teaching was always centered on other people, because that was the great commandment: Love God and your neighbor. People will recognize us as children of God not by all the goofy bumper stickers we have on our cars warning people that "if the rapture-happens-this-car-is-gonna-make-you-wreck." For some of us, there's no rapture required for that anyway! Rather, people will recognize us by our actions in serving. What are we known for? There's that question again. The disciples in this story recognized Jesus because of His actions, in how He called out to them, in how He told them how to fish for the thousandth time, and how the net didn't tear. I think in today's terms, we call those "indicators of the faith." Are we building a life where we're known for how we speak, or how we always cook for our friends and serve them, or by patiently teaching that one kid (like me) that one lesson over and over? Do we meet people's physical needs first before meeting their spiritual needs?

Not long ago I wrote in my Bible this note in Acts, "The church is Heaven on Earth; it is made up of those of us who are saved, not members of a building. You will know a true saint if, when you are with them, you feel as if you have touched Heaven."

This is what a community of grace looks like. It's determining a need, meeting it, and giving what is really needed. It's where we are known, loved, and accepted. We live in the middle of a broken world, and in this broken world we are to be active agents of grace and redemption. This is how we earn people's trust. There is community inside and outside the church. I think to become a strong missional church and serve our community outside the church, there needs to be a distinction in our minds about what servant-hood is. Being a servant isn't as self-satisfying as we think, or rewarding, or even comfortable. If you haven't sacrificed, you haven't really served. Serving is running an errand for the King. It's easy for us to serve each other in our little cliques, people we love. You don't have to ask me twice to be there for people I feel obliged to take care of. They are my family; of course I'm going to serve them. But in that same context, what if I become dissatisfied with the style of music at my church, and my preferences and desires are no longer met? What if there are too many "funny" people showing up at church lately? I've learned, and continue to learn, that church is more about meeting our Father and our family in God's big living room we call a sanctuary, where God is the leader, and we sing back to Him what He sings to our hearts. It's where we respond to His Words spoken through our pastor and where we throw ourselves at Jesus' feet when we bow at His altar. It's where we throw our arms around our family and put a balm on their wounds by taking them to our Father in the room and asking Him to help. That balm could be a song you didn't like. Everything about meeting in God's house is about Him and others.

I think the church building will always matter; while it's not the "Church," people will always think of the building as being a safe place to go and know that Jesus is there. Something I found to be true is that my generation values old church buildings and the history therein. It's like researching a family tree. They like tradition, because family has tradition. That's the cool thing about Portland's Door of Hope meeting in the old church building on 9th and Fremont; it was founded in 1902, and the first time I walked in the sanctuary I could feel that this was a place where worship has happened and that God had filled that place with Himself.

Josh, pastor of Door of Hope, has done some amazing remodeling, making it "Portland" unique but keeping the traditional appeal. I really loved the simplicity of the service. The music was just Josh playing the acoustic guitar, a piano, and maybe some drums. It felt more "authentic"; it is what my generation values. We don't need a "show" or concert with flashing lights. We need a truth encounter with the one who is truth. We need to hear Him speak and hear our praise go up to Him. In Portland, buildings and homes don't have air conditioning, because it's usually cool enough to do without. But it got so hot in that church that the windows were opened, spilling music and truth into the clean Portland air. There is a hunger for God when we pack into tiny hot sanctuaries. There is hunger for God when we are willing to stand in the back just to hear His Word.

It was at the intersection of Stark and 257 when I saw this young man standing on the corner with this sign that said, "YOU ARE LOVED!!" It was written in bright red paint. These words gripped my heart; a lump formed in my throat. I just had to meet this young man. What possessed him to do this? I parked my car at the closest gas station and made my way to him. My heart was overwhelmed. I told him I liked his sign and asked what encouraged him to do this. Nothing could have prepared me for his answer: "hatred for myself." Oh how I know that pain. I fought

tears. I looked at his arm, filled with cuts and scars, pain made visible. I

know that pain too. I choked. My new friend Philip elaborated and said, "I

feel like people don't see or hear these words enough, and I want to

make sure people know they are loved and to go share it." I think he's

right. This young man represents my generation well, the millennials.

Have you met us? Have you talked to us? We have a powerful story to tell

you. We need your love and your physical touch in our life. We are a

broken generation who are anxious, depressed, and sometimes even

suicidal. But we also believe in hope. We value relationships and very

much long for a sense of family from the church. We need for you to

listen to us and help us trust you. We need for you to ask us how we are

doing and how we connect with God. Our answer might surprise you. We

need to know that it matters. Ask us what our tattoos mean; ask us about

the scars on our wrist or arm. Tattoos have a lot of meaning to my

generation. It's literally a branding. We are branding our story; we are

branding Christ and our testimonies. We aren't as rebellious and angry as

you think. We have deep passions and convictions.

Are we worth loving? And even if we were angry and rebellious, love us where we are. Are we giving people the touch they need physically, emotionally, and spiritually? Do we love through listening? My generation longs for your relationship with us. We are kids who need you as the older generation help us grow up. Teach us to have a character that reflects Christ. God is working in us, but we need help to get it out of us. Show us; we'll watch and learn. We only know of God's love when the older generations reach out to us and love us right where we are. That's what this young man's cry was, a cry for love. Who is loving him? Does he know of God's love? I made my way back to my car, letting the tears flow as I walked. I thanked Jesus for Philip whose name means "friend and lover," and his boldness. What a mission for the church to meet. Love well, church. For the sake of the church, for the sake of Christ in all His love for us, for the sake of the Kingdom, love well.

How do we do this? I've sought God on this myself. I find myself desperate to get them to God, praying for years, patiently waiting. This is what the Lord gave me, and I hope it will help you as you are actively seeking and praying for your own list of people. We must commit, love, point toward, and bring them to God (Mark 2, Romans 12:9-21, 2

Thessalonians 2:11, Titus 2). This all must be done, sacrificially,

specifically, supernaturally, expectantly, excitingly, and endlessly.

CHAPTER TEN

On His Promises

"For all of God's promises have been fulfilled in Christ with a resounding "Yes!" And through Christ our "Amen!" (which means yes) ascends to God for His glory. It is God who enables us to stand firm for Christ in the commission He has given us through the Holy Spirit who is the installment guaranteeing the promise."

~2 Corinthians 1:20-22 [Paraphrased]

She grabbed my hand and said, "Listen!" Grabbing her hand back, I listened to the lyrics of the song that filled the sanctuary. I had heard the song hundreds of times, but this particular morning the lyrics were dumped straight into my heart. The lyrics that were all too familiar became new and alive again. She knew I needed to tune in and grasp the truth of these few words. God was speaking, and He was working. *He's not finished with me.* All the bad things I've done, He doesn't remember, and I'm not disqualified. Yet I sit chained to them some days, completely overwhelmed. David writes in Psalm 3, that the Lord is a shield against the enemy when he comes and tries to destroy. There are many who rise up and cause trouble and grief. Many try to keep me away from the Lord, saying "God can't help you!" But my Savior, He comes and rescues, the One who is my glory, and lifts my head, the One who watches over me when I sleep, the One in whom I find victory. He doesn't condemn me. He doesn't shame nor guilt me.

Psalm 19:12-14 says, *"How can I know all the sins lurking in my heart? Cleanse me from these hidden faults. Keep your servant from deliberate sins! Don't let them **control** me. Then I will be free of **guilt** and innocent of great sin. May the words of my mouth and the meditation of my heart be pleasing to you, O Lord, my rock and my redeemer."* Deliverance is found in this Psalm. Guilt cripples the Christ-follower and makes us fearful. But forgiveness is freedom.

You will recall the story of the woman who was caught in adultery and was brought before Jesus. By law, she was to be stoned. You can imagine her guilt and shame. She was called unworthy. Jesus didn't accuse her; He didn't condemn, but instead invited her to a life change. He extended forgiveness and the opportunity to turn from her sin. (John

8) God wasn't finished with her either. Jesus came to destroy the works of Satan and set us free once and for all. The power of the cross deactivated Satan's power over us. Yet, so often we forget and go right back into "jail"--so to speak.

God has already unlocked and broken the chains; we just have to let them go. On this journey, the One who we call "Savior," our Redeemer, holds us in His hand forever, He doesn't let go. Psalm 136 declares, "*His faithful love endures forever.*"

Today's generation of Christ-followers have the wrong definition of what it means to follow Christ in more ways than one. I'm thankful Jesus teaches us when we ask Him. We want to be "successful" Christians with big growing churches, a people who serve until we drop. We pour over articles full of "how-tos" and of what we're doing wrong in church so that maybe somehow, someway, someday we will be better and then maybe get a standing ovation from Jesus and the angels. It's exhausting. This, at least, is how my walk looks at times. But this is following what "religious" culture says we must do. I want to encourage you and tell you that you are enough. You are enough because of the Jesus in you. This is something I learned while in Portland. I've lived my life believing the lie that I'm not enough, that I'm just a waste of air and existence. My heart became overwhelmed to know that the God and Creator of this universe would think of me and loves me enough to come and live in me. That He would give Himself to me knowing that without Him, I could do nothing and that everything I tried to do apart from Him would mean nothing nor have lasting impact. He has promised Himself to us. And when we fling our arms around Him and call Him Lord and friend, He puts Himself in us to do life well.

There is one word this generation doesn't know: *rest*. God led me to study Hebrews 4, and in this passage of scripture it talks about a "keeping of the Sabbath." *Sabbatismos* is the Greek word used here, and it means that we are to enjoy an uninterrupted rest that is of God Himself so that a relationship with Him may take place. It refers to two kinds of rest: a rest now that is both spiritual and physical, and a rest to come that points to our eternal home of Heaven. *Resting now is a holy experience that produces holiness and perfects the work of Christ in us.* Rest is the one promise and gift from God many of us will never take as often as He gives. It says this in Hebrews 4:1-11:

"God's promise of entering his rest still stands, so we ought to tremble with fear that some of you might fail to experience it. 2 For this good news—that God has prepared this rest—has been announced to us just as it was to them. But it did them no good because they didn't share the faith of those who listened to God. 3 For only we who believe can enter his rest. As for the others, God said, "In my anger I took an oath: 'They will never enter my place of rest', even though this rest has been ready since he made the world. 4 We know it is ready because of the place in the Scriptures where it mentions the seventh day: "On the seventh day God rested from all his work." 5 But in the other passage God said, "They will never enter my place of rest." 6 So God's rest is there for people to enter, but those who first heard this good news failed to enter because they disobeyed God. 7 So God set another time for entering his rest, and that time is today. God announced this through David much later in the words already quoted: "Today when you hear his voice, don't harden your hearts." 8 Now

if Joshua had succeeded in giving them this rest, God would

not have spoken about another day of rest still to come. 9

So there is a special rest still waiting for the people of God.

10 For all who have entered into God's rest have rested

from their labors, just as God did after creating the world.

11 So let us do our best to enter that rest. But if we disobey

God, as the people of Israel did, we will fall."

This rest is a part of the Good News of Christ, the truth that Jesus is enough and that if we never did another single thing but put our full trust in Him it would be enough. Trust/faith is rest. When we believe in Him, we have given up our works and the things that we think will make us better before God or will make us more accepting to Him. We trust that God through Jesus Christ and His finished work on the cross has already accepted us. It means we are free, no longer slaves working to be enough. This is a rest of grace that is full, blessed, sweet, satisfying, and peaceful. Slaves don't rest, but free people do, and we are a free people. What's so beautiful about this passage of scripture from Hebrews is that the author is pointing back to Joshua and of the rest promised to the

Israelites as they entered the Promised Land. It says in Joshua 21:43-45 this:

> "So the Lord gave to Israel all the land he had sworn to give their ancestors, and they took possession of it and settled there. 44 And the Lord gave them rest on every side, just as he had solemnly promised their ancestors. None of their enemies could stand against them, for the Lord helped them conquer all their enemies. 45 **Not a single one of all the good promises the Lord had given to the family of Israel was left unfulfilled; everything he had spoken came true."**

Our lives and our journeys can be compared to the Israelites roaming in the desert for all those years just trying to get to the Promised Land...a land of rest. We, too, are lost in deserts; times of rest seems so far away, but I am reminded that even in their wandering they still rested, and God still provided for every need they had. We, too, must lean into the rest promised now and must rely on the promise of Heaven. I love the last verse of the passage; everything the Lord has spoken came to pass. He doesn't forget His people, and we are His people--those of us who trust in His name and call Him Father and Lord. I feel like He is warning me not to harden my heart like Israel did in the wilderness. Though they had left Egypt, a place of unrest, they often longed to go back. They stubbornly refused to trust the Lord completely. They wanted the old way life; oppressive and disappointing as it all was, there was still an alluring appeal. Unbelief forfeits rest.

It is His will that we rest, and yet I'm not obedient to His rest; I don't have the faith to rest. I fear that it will all fall apart and there will be no recovery. But there are moments when I feel the presence of God Himself come down and meet with me where I am, and He reminds me that life without rest is vanity. In the quest to live above the sun with God and an eternal perspective and not what I can just see today...it's then that He brings me up into His lap and wraps His arms around me and pulls me into His chest and He sings me a hymn as I drift to sleep...rest. It gives me an eternal perspective that assures me that everything is going to be okay, and that this is all temporary and doesn't compare to the land He has promised to take me. There is no place I would rather be, but the alluring appeal of the world and old ways creeps in, and takes me from this rest. Resting is a learned action, one only learned from Jesus who is the definition of rest.

Many times when we share our testimony with others, we are focusing all on what we used to be and go on and on about how bad we were before we got saved. However, in doing this, the emphasis is not on Jesus at all. The emphasis is on Satan and his evil schemes. This brought me to think about Noah and the flood. Imagine Noah writing down his story and putting all the emphasis on the flood. Forty days and forty nights it rained; he was stuck on a boat with smelly animals and his family. God destroyed pretty much all of mankind, sparing only Noah and his family. Then the earth got dry, and we were thankful God saved us… "the end." The story does not end that way though; it ends with Noah giving a sacrifice of praise to God and God giving Noah a promise. In thinking about how we approach our lives and the testimonies God has allowed us to endure, do we compose our stories to give God glory or Satan? Do we just end with Jesus saving us? We end up missing God's promises in our lives because we cling to what was and not what is, which is a sacrifice of praise and a better life God offers. If there is one thing that has stuck with me about His promises it is this: "The promises of God are more about the promiser than the promise itself." Everything about our lives point to Jesus. He is everything, the author, perfector, finisher, and lover of our lives. We give Satan a lot more credit than what he is worth when it comes to spiritual warfare. Satan can't see our future; he can't wreck God's plan for our lives...unless God or we let him. When things go wrong, it's not always Satan out to get us. He can only be in one place at one time. He isn't omnipresent or omnipotent. He can't get in our head and read our thoughts; we belong to Christ.

I had just moved to Portland, and it rained mostly toward the end of the day. As the evening came to end, my friend called me outside. I looked up, and there was the most beautiful rainbow in the sky. As I had been clinging to His promises in this time of transition, I took much peace in seeing this. It is as if God Himself had come down to earth on His throne just to be near us and assure us, *I've not forgotten you, see here my promise remains*. This rainbow is ever before Him in His presence on His throne. It is an ever faithful, eternal covenant between creation and Creator and is still intact to this very day to this generation.

"Covenant" means a long-term relationship. As God called me to Portland, and as I have prayed for this city, praying for their salvation, asking for God to move, He gives me His rainbow--His promise over

Portland, to His people; He is mighty to save! Oswald Chambers says this in his devotional, *My Utmost for His Highest*:

> "It is the will of God that human beings should get into a right-standing relationship with Him, and His covenants are designed for this purpose. Why doesn't God save me? He has accomplished and provided for my salvation, but I have not yet entered into a relationship with Him. Why doesn't God do everything we ask? He has done it. The point is— will I step into that covenant relationship? All the great blessings of God are finished and complete, but they are not mine until I enter into a relationship with Him on the basis of His covenant."

Covenants are about God's work of redeeming us back to Himself from sin. The covenants God made with His people highlight the humanity of our condition, our brokenness, our role as bearing the image of God, our suffering, and our calling. There are five elements to a covenant, the people and mediator representing the people, the blessing, the condition of receiving, the sign of the promise, and the result of what the covenant is structurally doing in the Jesus family. There are six major covenants in the Bible that God made with His people. Noah was one of them. The sixth and final Covenant is called "The New Covenant" (Matthew 26:26-30), where Jesus in our mediator and the blessing is His finished work on the cross. If we believe in Him, if we receive His blood into our lives, we are welcomed into relationship with God through Jesus. The sign of our covenant relationship is communion. It's so beautiful; I used to feel depressed every time communion came around. It seemed more like a funeral, and you're the murderer in the room; I felt like I killed Jesus in a shameful kind of way...just a heavy feeling. Maybe it's supposed to feel that way, but the more I get to know Jesus and His Word and the way He works, communion should be a time of celebration and remembering the whole story of the cross and His shed blood for us. It's true that my sin put Jesus on the cross, and it should have been me. But God's love couldn't bear that thought. When I take the bread and cup of His body and blood broken and shed for me, I remember that He finished and destroyed the power of sin, that I'm forgiven and loved. I remember that I don't have to have it all together, because the Jesus in me does. The truth is that Jesus stepped down out of Heaven willingly as the second Adam to finish what He knew we couldn't do. It also fulfilled the promises and past covenants He had made.

As a result, He made us His Church, the Bride of Jesus himself! It's the promise that He is going to come sweeping in like Prince Charming and carry us off into the sunset to His Kingdom where we live happily ever after. And even better, this covenant is extended to the gentiles...the entire world! This is the beginning of missions as we know it to be. Pre-cross Peter confessed Jesus as the Christ, Son of the living God. Jesus assured Peter that He would build His church upon what Peter just confessed and believed. Giving him the keys to the Kingdom, He promised that the powers of Hell would not conquer it. We got the keys! Any time we get a key to something, it is special and significant. It indicates a certain maturity has been reached, a readiness to be privileged and trusted with the responsibility to carry and have possession of those keys. Keys open and close things in our lives; they lock and unlock. We have keys to our car, to our home, to valuable things, to our work places. They can indicate power and status. It is power to get into a place that no one else can unless they too hold that unique key.

That's why God gave us gifts; they are keys to the Kingdom, and that's why we are called a body. We all function differently. My hands can't see; only my eyes see. This, too, is something I'm still learning; I

can't tell you how many times my spiritual mother in the Lord has

preached this to me until she's blue in the face (I have that effect on

people). It's finally sticking. Paul explains to his spiritual children at

Corinth in 1 Corinthians 12:

> "There are different kinds of spiritual gifts, but the same Spirit is
>
> the source of them all. **5** There are different kinds of service, but
>
> we serve the same Lord. **6** God works in different ways, but it is
>
> the same God who does the work in all of us.
>
> **7** A spiritual gift is given to each of us so we can help each other. **8**
>
> To one person the Spirit gives the ability to give wise advice; to
>
> another the same Spirit gives a message of special knowledge. **9**
>
> The same Spirit gives great faith to another, and to someone else
>
> the one Spirit gives the gift of healing. **10** He gives one person the
>
> power to perform miracles, and another the ability to prophesy.
>
> He gives someone else the ability to discern whether a message is
>
> from the Spirit of God or from another spirit. Still another person is
>
> given the ability to speak in unknown languages, while another is
>
> given the ability to interpret what is being said. **11** It is the one

and only Spirit who distributes all these gifts. He alone decides which gift each person should have."

God gave you special "powers" by His very own deciding and assigning, and nobody in this world can do what He has gifted you to do like you. While other people may have your same skills and gifts, they aren't you. Your uniqueness is in how you treat those you serve, perhaps in how you treat co-workers. My two most recent jobs have been scooping frozen yogurt and working at a land surveying company. It seems like a pretty ordinary job, but the uniqueness is in who owns the company: ultimately, God. The people I work for in these places are people who seek to honor Jesus and very much see their companies as a ministry in building the Kingdom.

What I want you to know is that, with Jesus, you can never fail, because He never fails! After Jesus sealed His covenant with His disciples, they sang a hymn. It is thought that Psalm 136 was sung that night as Jesus was about to go to the cross. Thankfulness always precedes the miracle. Worship Him with me:

1 Give thanks to the Lord, for he is good!

His faithful love endures forever.

2 Give thanks to the God of gods.

His faithful love endures forever.

3 Give thanks to the Lord of lords.

His faithful love endures forever.

4 Give thanks to him who alone does mighty miracles.

His faithful love endures forever.

5 Give thanks to him who made the heavens so skillfully.

His faithful love endures forever.

6 Give thanks to him who placed the earth among the waters.

His faithful love endures forever.

7 Give thanks to him who made the heavenly lights—

His faithful love endures forever.

8 the sun to rule the day,

His faithful love endures forever.

9 and the moon and stars to rule the night.

His faithful love endures forever.

10 Give thanks to him who killed the firstborn of Egypt.
His faithful love endures forever.
11 He brought Israel out of Egypt.
His faithful love endures forever.
12 He acted with a strong hand and powerful arm.
His faithful love endures forever.

13 Give thanks to him who parted the Red Sea.[a]

His faithful love endures forever.

14 He led Israel safely through,

His faithful love endures forever.

15 but he hurled Pharaoh and his army into the Red Sea.

His faithful love endures forever.

16 Give thanks to him who led his people through the wilderness.

His faithful love endures forever.

17 Give thanks to him who struck down mighty kings.

His faithful love endures forever.

18 He killed powerful kings—

His faithful love endures forever.

19 Sihon king of the Amorites,

His faithful love endures forever.

20 and Og king of Bashan.

His faithful love endures forever.

21 God gave the land of these kings as an inheritance—

His faithful love endures forever.

22 a special possession to his servant Israel.

His faithful love endures forever.

23 He remembered us in our weakness.

His faithful love endures forever.

24 He saved us from our enemies.

His faithful love endures forever.

25 He gives food to every living thing.

His faithful love endures forever.

26 Give thanks to the God of heaven.

His faithful love endures forever.

ABOUT THE AUTHOR

Allison resides in Charlotte, North Carolina with her family. Her hobbies include writing, playing music, and spending time outdoors. She has a love for cows. After graduating from High School in 2008, she attended Central Piedmont Community College. She is the Founder of *Living Above the Sun Ministries* which seeks to empower all generations and people to find their purpose in life by setting their vision to living from an eternal perspective. A vision God gave her in 2012, she has worked to develop this ministry using the gifts God has given her through writing, music, and teaching.

THE TOOLS OF OUR TRADE
BIBLE STUDY
FURTHER TRAINING IN HOW TO USE OUR TOOLS

Our way is always rebellion, God's way is always our repentance from our way. In this study we will look at, and contrast our way and God's way. This is a study, and work of repentance in knowing God's heart, and using the gifts He has given to walk in His way.

PART ONE: I BOW LOW
THE GIFT OF RIGHTEOUSNESS AND PEACE

Rebellion and Repentance- *"we capture their rebellious thoughts, and teach them to obey Christ."*

The rebellion of our way is the pride of self worship that leads to destruction.

The end result of our repentance is a humbleness of worshiping Him that leads to obedience.

This is accomplished by capturing the rebellion of pride and self making it bow and obey God in His way in humbleness. Leading to a life of right living in the redemption of Jesus' blood.

Our Authority in Christ- *"having authority given by Christ, we use it to build you up, and not down."*

The only way to capture and overpower an idea is with an even better idea. And the idea in this case is the idea that God made us for Himself. This is what life in Christ has always been about since the beginning. God is in the work of restoring, and redeeming us back to Himself we we fell from Him. Our purpose and structure in life is the truth of:

Tools of Our Trade- *"we use God's mighty weapons, not the worlds."*

~Our WORSHIP isn't just for anyone or anything, we were designed to be worshiping creatures. Our worship is for God alone.

~When we SPEAK HIS NAME it is to not be in vain, or in cursing. We speak His name when we are speaking to Him, or of Him. It is the highest name in all the world. To hold it on our tongue is of the utmost honor and privilege.

~Our LOVE is made perfect in Him who loved us first. We do not know love, or how to love until Jesus puts His love in us. He is love. It's more than we could ever know.

~UNIFIED as one, because we are better together, we all belong to each other. We tend to want to unify for a cause, but exclude. Under the cross and body of Christ we become unified and one, bound in love that cannot be broken.

Lessons from the Word- *Jonah*

Read the Book of Jonah.

Appointed- ordained with a purpose. Produce fruit, but more so, produce fruit with seed!

To proclaim God's wrath, and judgment if Nineveh did not repent.

The whale, weed, and seas obeyed God.

Jonah's pride was that he thought Nineveh deserved to be destroyed. Jonah wanted to stay in his homeland with his people.

We cannot save ourselves. Not by strength, not by getting rid of all the bad stuff in our lives, and not by works.

Salvation is: believing what God says is true, obeying His commandments, this is accomplished through and by repentance.

The Gospel results in the Righteousness and Peace of God.

<u>Repentance</u>- *"If my people will humble themselves and pray, seeking my face turning from their ways"*

Worship-

Love-

"Now the Word of the Lord came to _____ saying, 'Arise, and go to_____, and preach the message I will give you.'"

Will you obey?

<u>Walk it Out</u>- *"those who claim to live in Him, must walk as Jesus did."*

In the Light of His Love.

Read Ephesians 5:1-14.

<u>The Key</u>-

Prayer

Read John 17.

It's all for His glory and name.

Because there is power in His name.

We are sanctified; set-apart by the truth of His Word.

That we would know Him, and be in Him. To be loved by Him.

Though the world hates us, we are full of His joy.

His prayer is for us, not against us.

All of this we believe, and commit to finishing the work He has given.

My repentance is my obedience; using the God-tools of Righteousness and Peace.

PART TWO: I LIVE ABOVE THE SUN, THE GIFT OF SALVATION AND FAITH

Rebellion and Repentance- *"we capture their rebellious thoughts, and teach them to obey Christ."*

The rebellion of our way is the philosophies of good works that lead to judgment.

The end result of our repentance is the wisdom of commission that leads to assurance.

This is accomplished by capturing the rebellious philosophies and good works structuring it to the wisdom and commission of Jesus. An eternal view that assures Salvation through faith.

Our Authority in Christ- *"having authority given by Christ, we use it to build you up, and not down."*

The idea of Kingdom order and rule by King Jesus, who chose us to do His mission in the World. We are called, chosen, and faithful to this mission to bring many to the Kingdom.

<u>The Tools of Our Trade</u>- *"we use God's mighty weapons, not the worlds."*

Our <u>MIND</u> and the way we think; obtaining the mind of who we serve

Our <u>HEART</u> and who we love and are loyal to

Our <u>WILL</u>, the wants and desires we entertain.

<u>Lessons From the Word</u>- Joab- 2 Samuel &1 Kings

<u>Loyal</u> but lost.

Joab's actions were not <u>authorized</u> by King David. His actions were to his own <u>glory</u>, and achievement.

We are not saved by <u>loyalty</u>, <u>right belief</u>, or <u>risking our life</u>.

God wants our <u>heart</u> and <u>surrender</u>.

Not to just be a <u>hearer</u> of **HIS Word**, but be a <u>doer</u> of **HIS Word**.

This is **NOT** <u>busyness</u>!

This **IS** <u>obedience</u> to what He has <u>commanded</u>!

<u>Repentance</u>- *"If my people will humble themselves and pray, seeking my*

face turning from their ways"

Busyness-

Lack of obedience-

Being a "Joab"-

Are you with Jesus?

Walk it Out- *"those who claim to live in Him, must walk as Jesus did."*

In Wisdom

Read Ephesians 5:15-21; Proverbs 1-4.

The Key-

His Mission, and Authority

Read Matthew 28:19-22; Daniel 7:13-14

There is one name by which we are saved, Jesus.

Who has been given all authority in Heaven and Earth.

The wisdom is in the Authority of Jesus Christ.

Wisdom is what comes from above, and knowledge is what we gather in our observations surrounding us. Vertical versus horizontal.

His _mind_ is that we would go, make disciples in His authority and sending.

His _heart_ is that he is with us, always, until the end.

His _will_ is that we would baptize, teach what Jesus taught, and obey it!

Though I once _doubted_, my _repentance_ is in my _assurance_.

Using the God tools of _Salvation_ and _faith_.

I _believe_ and _surrender_ myself to His mission.

PART THREE: I STAND FIRM,
THE GIFT OF TRUTH

<u>Rebellion and Repentance</u>- *"we capture their rebellious thoughts, and teach them to obey Christ."*

Destroying the rebellion of manipulation and unfaithfulness to the Truth of God's Word, and to each other. Re-Building lives of authenticity and love, allowing a firm foundation to stand faithfully for God.

<u>Our Authority in Christ</u>- *"having authority given by Christ, we use it to build you up, and not down."*

The idea that our individual lives shape another into future generations. in the form of: Our family and our children, our church family, and our Culture. We are used through and by the Spirit to fulfill the work He had planned for us before the World was made.

<u>The Tools of Our Trade</u>- *"we use God's mighty weapons, not the worlds."*

God has gifted us with <u>natural characteristics, and abilities.</u> In this we make up the body of the Church in fulfilling our distinct role.

<u>The Bible</u> is the infallible Word of God, it is our sword in which we fight. His Word when it is spoken will not return void.

Lessons from the Word- *Esther*

Read the book of Esther.

Esther found <u>favor</u> with the King through her <u>natural</u> beauty.

God has a purpose and plan for me that no one else can <u>fulfill</u>, for such a <u>time</u> as this.

In Esther we see Jesus, the <u>advocate</u> who stands in <u>boldness</u> pleading for the life of her people, The <u>Jews</u>.

There is a battle of <u>two</u> kingdoms seen in <u>Mordecai</u> and <u>Haman</u>. Heaven and Hell, Light and Dark, Christ and Satan.

Manipulation, and unfaithfulness leads to a life of no reward, and no blessing.

No weapon formed against me shall prosper. We are sealed by the Holy Spirit.

"for whatever is written in the king's name and sealed with the king's signet ring no one can revoke." (8:8)

Today we are still reading of Esther's courage to save her people. The Jews still celebrate the feast of Purim to remember their rescuing. See Esther 9:28

Repentance- *"If my people will humble themselves and pray, seeking my face turning from their ways"*

Where has God placed you for such a time as this? Are you being faithful to it?

Are you content sitting back watching Satan destroy our people? What will you do?

Are you manipulating the of the Word of God? Do you leave certain parts out because you don't think it will go over well?

Are you remaining silent?

Will you teach your children and future generations of the ways of the

Lord?

What legacy will you leave?

Walk it Out- *"those who claim to live in Him, must walk as Jesus did."*

In Unity

Read Ephesians 4:1-16.

The Key

His Word

Read 2 Timothy 3:10-17; Romans 15:4,8.

2 Timothy 3:16 starts with ALL SCRIPTURE- This verse can be the very crux

of the Bible. Passing every scripture through this verse asking the

questions:

>What doctrine is being taught?

>What is the correction where I may be wrong?

>What is the challenge? Where do I need more practice, and strengthening?

>What truth is being gained?

By the God breathed scriptures we have persevered, and felt His comfort.

We have hope, because Jesus Christ has ministered to us the truth of God, and has spoken yes and amen to confirm the promises made.

Though manipulation seems to grow more and more, we have been equipped and know His word.

His Word is our completion, and causes us to be faithful.

My faithfulness is my repentance, using the God tool of Truth.On that day, when Heaven fills my sight, and the presence of Jesus surrounds me, He will look me in the eyes and say: Well done my good and faithful servant, great is your reward.

Made in the USA
Columbia, SC
30 August 2021